Success
Corruption
& Lies

The Cure

By Ross Clarke

s u c c

c o r r u

a n d

KINGSFLEET
PUBLICATIONS

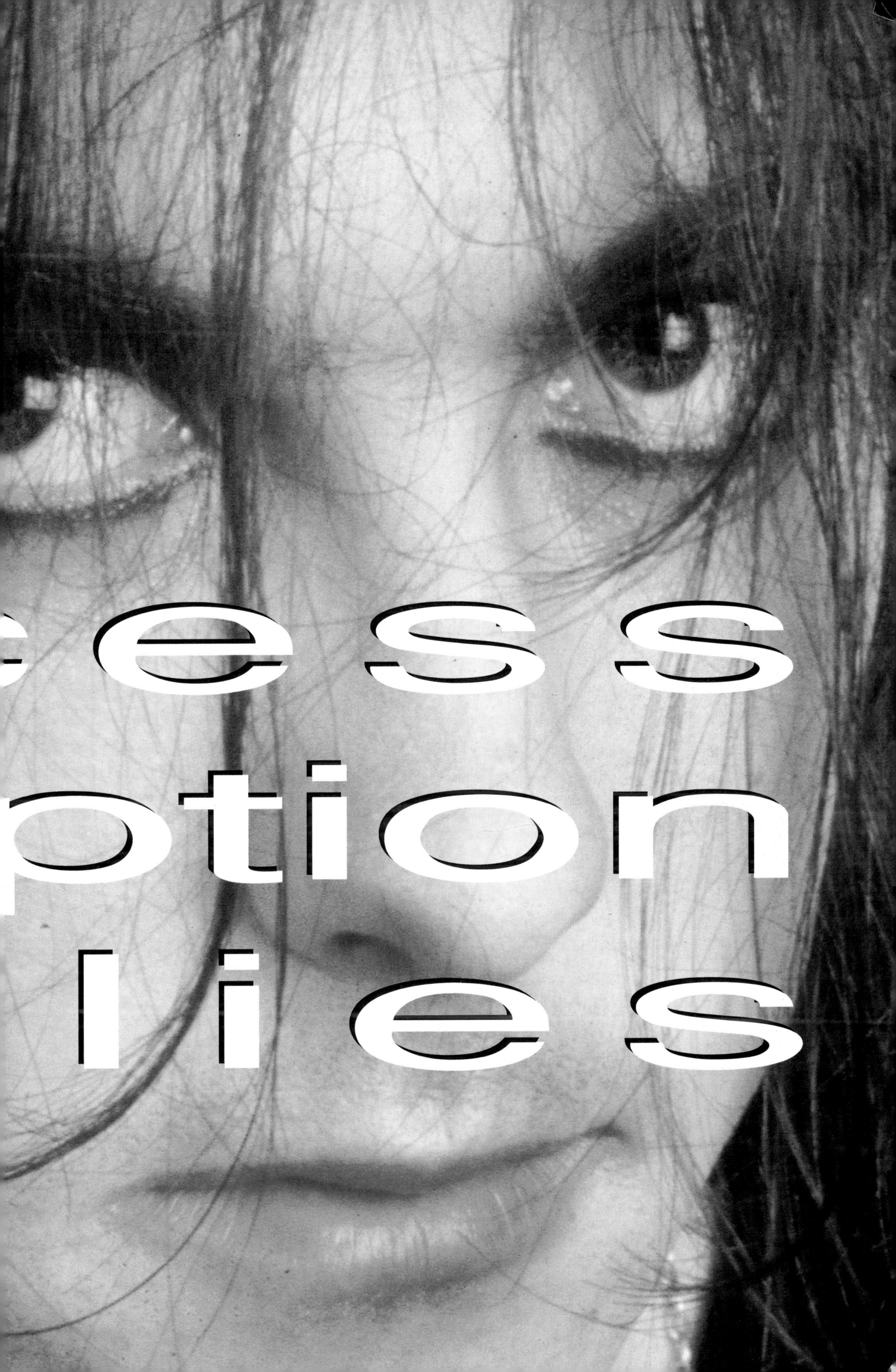
ess
ption
lies

contents

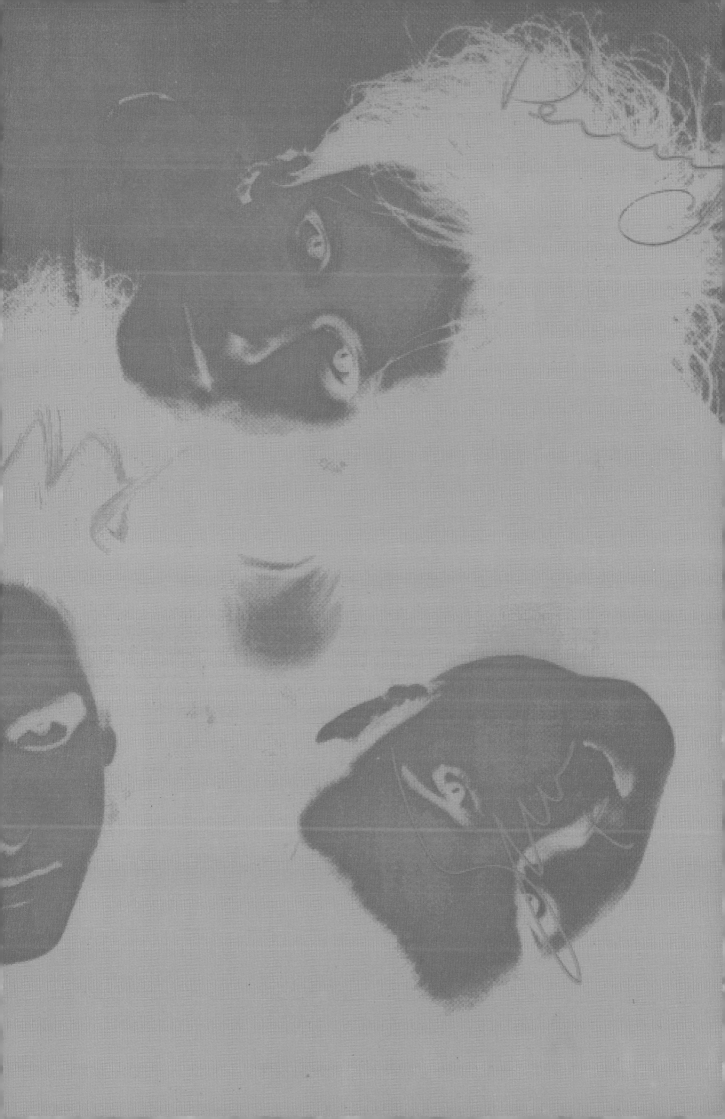

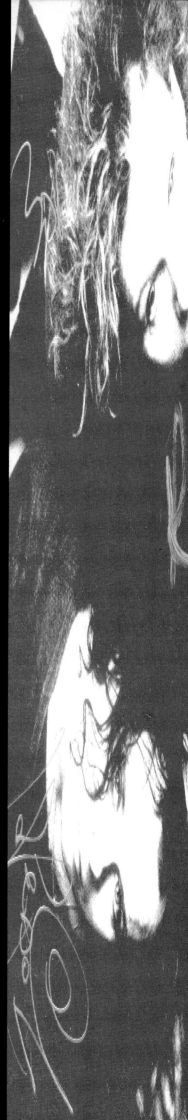

the
cure

In 1977, if anyone had been laying odds on a band becoming a huge success, The Cure wouldn't even have figured in the reckoning. Back then, it seemed incredible that the outfit which had been formed that year, in the unlikely setting of the commuter-belt sprawl of Crawley in West Sussex, by four schoolboys would, later become one of the most successful bands in the UK and a top-line attraction around the world.

Their meteoric rise to megastardom, however, has not been without years of hard graft and, in those years, The Cure have received their fair share of critical ridicule. They have been labelled miserable, facile, introspective, esoteric, arrogant, angst-ridden and tortured. In their early days they certainly were. They were anti-image, anti-rock 'n' roll and arguably the band that helped begin the 'gloom

HAPPINESS

movement', gaining a large cult following as they did so.

In the mid-Eighties, despite allegations from hard-core fans that they had 'sold out', their music became more accessible, more commercial, if no less delirious, and they shot into the pop charts and into the glare of the public spotlight. The Cure left their cult status behind and never looked back. In the Nineties, The Cure's popularity shows no sign of waning - paradoxically, each year seems to yield a fresh perspective on the band known for it's flashes of quirky, individualistic humour.

The enigmatic leading light of The Cure, Robert James Smith, was born in Blackpool on 21st April 1959. His family relocated to Crawley in West Sussex when he was a small child and it was here he spent his formative years. Whilst he was at St. Francis' Primary

FORGETTING THE LIMITS OF YOUR OWN EXISTENCE IF ONLY FOR A MOMENT...

school he met Cure co-founder
Lawrence 'Lol' Tolhurst although, by all
accounts, it wasn't until 1972 that they
first spoke to each other.

Although he had only spent a few years
in Blackpool, he was blessed with a
northern accent due to his parents' own
strong Lancashire tones. In the
southern county of Sussex, this stuck
out like a sore thumb and he felt
somewhat removed from his
schoolmates. It wasn't until he was in
his early teens and attending the Notre
Dame Middle School that he realised
that it was probably his accent that held
him apart from the rest and he
managed to tone it down, although the
other pupils probably regarded Robert
wearing a black velvet dress to school
for a dare as strange as his accent!

Rebelling against the school's
fundamental Catholic principals, Robert

began playing guitar in earnest as this allowed him to spend time in the music room instead of attending the rigourous religious education lessons. This he did with his mates Lol Tolhurst and Michael Dempsey who also found spending time making music far more pleasurable than attending class. At the end of their final year at the school, they were expected to make public their musical education and played a piece to the class calling themselves The Obelisks. Robert played piano, Lol played drums, and Michael played guitar along with fellow absconders Alan Hill on bass and Marc Ceccagno also handling the guitar parts. Robert later admitted "It was horrible! But much better than studying!"

At the age of thirteen they all moved on to

St. Wilfred's Comprehensive school. If they had found the free-thinking, revolutionary Notre Dame restricting, they must have found this educational institution positively suffocating. St Wilfred's had strict ideas on discipline and it didn't take much time for Robert and Marc Ceccagno to find themselves suspended by the ruling authorities for being an 'undesirable influence' although they were later reinstated.

here was no chance of skipping class to create music, horrible or otherwise, at this establishment. No sir! Any rebellious forms of recreation such as forming a band had to be done strictly outside school hours and this is exactly what they did. On 23rd January 1976 they held their first band rehearsal in St. Edward's Church hall.

The line-up consisted of Robert and Marc on guitars, Michael on bass and a drummer called Graham. Graham had been admitted into this select circle of anarchists because he possessed a drum kit. Graham's brother had an amp and a microphone, so he was immediately enlisted to provide the vocals.

The group rehearsed once a week and called themselves Malice. Some months later it had become apparent that the anonymous singer's vocal ability was distinctly lacking, and he was asked to leave. His brother left in hot pursuit, taking with him the much-needed drum kit. This left Malice in somewhat of a dilemma - no vocalist and no drummer. Lol immediately grasped this opportunity and convinced the others that he could be the drummer. Lol's inclusion in

the band roughly coincided with Marc leaving it because he was more interested in playing jazz. Malice's repertoire at this time consisted of Bowie, Hendrix and Alex Harvey covers which were not really to Marc's taste. He was replaced by a friend of Lol's named Porl Thompson.

They soon started writing their own material and, on 18 December 1976, they played their debut gig at Worth Abbey in Sussex. It was an acoustic set, reportedly with all four of them sitting on the floor playing bongos! Two days later, Malice supported Marc Ceccagno's newly formed Amulet at St. Wilfred's school. They had recruited a journalist with The Crawley Observer to provide the vocals. He arrived at the gig wearing a three-piece suit, a Manchester United scarf and a motorcycle helmet which appeared welded to his head - he refused to

remove it because he feared it would be stolen. He was probably quite wise to keep it on as his renditions of 'Jailbreak', 'Suffragette City' and 'Foxy Lady' did not go down at all well with the audience. Out of the three hundred present, two hundred left the auditorium and the remainder climbed on to the stage. It is sufficient to say that Martin's vocal services were not called on again by the band.

hen Robert left St. Wilfred's in 1977 with two A-levels, his parents were keen that he should follow his brother to university. This, however, was a time when punk had gripped the nation in its anarchistic, rebellious talons and Robert found the idea of three more years of discipline unpalatable. He later commented: "The liberation of punk for us was the sense that you didn't have to be orthodox...a sense of total release."

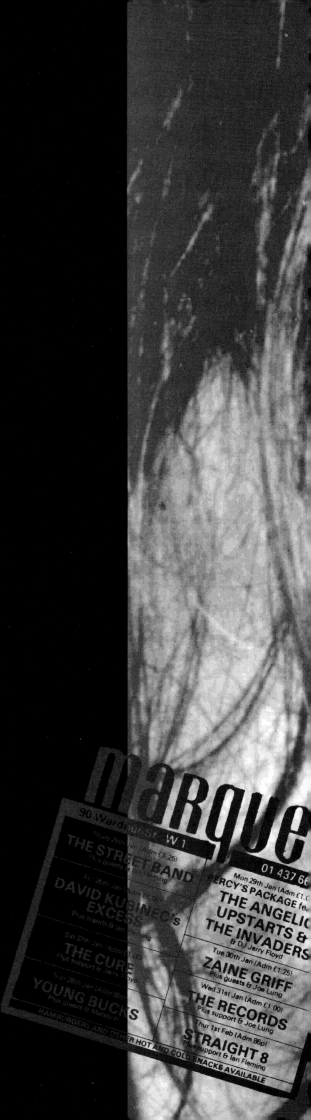

he band had now been reduced to Michael on bass, Robert handling the guitar parts and Lol on a finally acquired drum kit. They proceeded to rehearse three or four times a week in an annexe at Robert's house. Robert revealed later in 'Ten Imaginary Years', an official Cure biography: "The group was a way of doing something. I didn't hope for anything, but I found our songs better than those I was listening to. My biggest influence at that time was John Peel. From the age of 15, I used to listen to his show every night, that was the best part of the day. I heard White Riot and cut off all my hair! The Buzzcocks, The Stranglers...I used to dream of making a record that John Peel would play.

"We decided we needed another name if we were going to start playing again, so one night in January 1977, we sat around in my kitchen discussing it. One of our songs was called 'Easy Cure', a song written by Lol and, eventually, in desperation, we settled on that."

By this time it had become apparent to the music industry that punk, which had initially so shocked the business, was not going to go away. The whole punk movement was in full swing and being whole-heartedly embraced by the majority of the younger generation. What started as Malcolm McLaren's 'great rock 'n' roll swindle' was growing in popularity and record companies were all desperately searching for their own punk band.

 Most major record companies have whole departments whose sole aim in life is to seek out new talent, either by scouring clubs and pubs or by tirelessly sifting through hundreds of demo tapes per week. However, the German-based label Hansa, which was at that time distributed by Ariola in the UK, tried to short-cut this painstaking procedure and organised a talent contest which was advertised in the music press. The winner would receive an exclusive recording deal with the label. Easy Cure spotted the advert and recorded their entry on a tape recorder using vocalist Peter O'Toole. They were surprised but delighted to receive a telegram a few days later inviting them to audition at Morgan Studios in London on 13 May. After running through a couple of their songs in front of a video camera, they were offered a five-year recording deal and an advance of £1,000. The band were ecstatic. Robert stated optimistically at the time: "It all happened so fast, but now we are really looking forward to making our first record."

They had only been in existence for eight months and had no time to perfect their playing or their songwriting, so to have obtained a recording contract so early in their career, in a business in which there are literally thousands of young hopefuls and very few success stories, was an impressive achievement. The deal proved, however, to be more of a millstone than an open door to stardom.

Over the next three months, Easy Cure began gigging locally in small pubs and clubs and started to build up quite a following. They played a free gig at a Peace concert in Queen's Square, Crawley to an audience of 300 and were reviewed for the first time by the local press.

SONG

THE BEST CURE FOR MOST THINGS IS SING

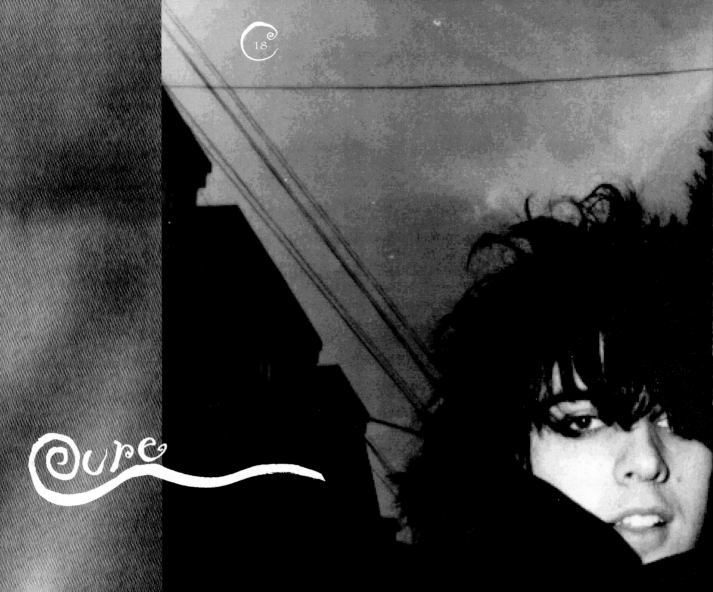

Cure

In September, vocalist Peter O'Toole decided that music was not his vocation in life and quit the band, preferring instead to spend his time on a Kibbutz in Israel. Robert, tired of the continually changing line-up and the constant stream of untalented singers that had moved through the ranks of the band, decided to take the vocals on himself.

O n 11th October the band went into SAV studios in London and recorded their first quality demo. Tracks recorded during these sessions included: 'See The Children', 'I Just Need Myself', 'I Want To Be Old', 'Pillbox Tales', 'Meathook', 'Rebel Rebel', 'I Saw Her Standing There', 'I'm Cold', 'Little Girl' and 'Killing An Arab'. The Bowie covers were included at the insistence of their label, Hansa, as Lol Tolhurst revealed later to Melody Maker.

"They'd give us the money to do demos and suggest a couple of things for us to do - they suggested we do a couple of Bowie tunes, for instance. We'd do that and put about four or five songs of our own as well. They'd get past the first one and say, 'This is horrible - not even people in prison would like this!' Then we wouldn't hear from them again."

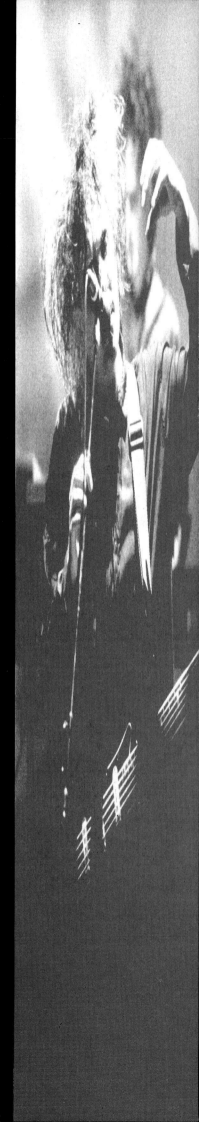

ansa hated the tracks that Easy Cure recorded and, in January 1978, they were sent to PSL studios with producer Trevor Vallis to record more demos. Robert recalled: "They were giving us all these old songs to cover. We couldn't believe it. This was 1978 and we thought we'd be able to do all these new songs we'd written and all they wanted from us were versions of really banal old rock 'n' roll songs…"

"Anyway, they said 'This is your last chance boys', so we went in and did 'Plastic Passion', 'I Just Need Myself', 'Rebel Rebel' and 'Smashed Up' - the worst song we ever recorded. The only remarkable thing about the whole day was that Lol got knocked over by a bus! We had to spend a couple of hours holding him up in the pub, pouring brandy down his throat. He spent the rest of the day playing drums and bleeding.

"On top of all this I had suddenly realised that I actually hated the songs we were doing and that, even if Hansa liked them, we wouldn't follow through."

obert had no need to worry, Hansa rejected these tracks as well. The label bosses were at a loss to know what to do with Easy Cure. They looked good - they were young and cute, they had a certain 'something' but it would have paid Hansa to remember that they were very young and inexperienced and both their playing and songwriting skills were underdeveloped. A band at this stage of their career needs nurturing, direction and a great deal of time spent understanding their psychology. Hansa appeared to have ignored this strategy and, as a result, the union was far from satisfactory.

t the end of March, their marriage with Hansa ended in divorce when the band suggested 'Killing An Arab' should be released as a single. Hansa thought the song was in bad taste and refused. They also terminated the band's contract, a move which must have been somewhat of a relief to both parties. On the positive side, the experience with Hansa had enabled the band to buy a new PA, given them some much-needed studio experience as well as a providing them with a reasonable retainer from which they could live and maintain the band. In addition to this, Robert had cleverly ensured that the copyright to all the original songs reverted to the band, so they had a high quality demo tape, paid for by Hansa, into the bargain.

The Hansa advance had also provided the band with some new equipment, although Robert's choice reflected the feel of the songs that were to come. He bought a Bon Tempi organ, a Top 20 guitar from Woolworths, purchased for £20, and a little WEM amp in an attempt to recreate the feel of Costello's less-is-more 'My Aim Is True'. Whilst he was busy minimalising the songs, so the line-up also contracted. Guitarist Porl Thompson left the band and Easy Cure became a trio. As if to

ADMIRATION

NOT KNOWING; JUST HOPING

SONGWORDS 1978-1989
the Cure

compliment the line-up, the band's name was also shortened. Robert later explained: "I had always thought Easy Cure was a bit hippyish, a bit American sounding, a bit West Coast, and I hated it, which put Lol's back up as he'd thought of it. Every other group we had liked had 'The' in front of their name but The Easy Cure sounded stupid so we just changed it to The Cure instead. It upset a few old fans but..well, there you are...I thought The Cure sounded much more it."

There followed sporadic gigs around their home town of Crawley and another recording session, financed by a mate, this time in Chestnut, a small eight-track studio in Sussex. They recorded four songs including: 'Boys Don't Cry', '10.15', 'It's Not You' and 'Fire In Cairo'. Accompanied by a letter and photograph, these demos were sent to all the major record companies. The tape fell on deaf ears (or probably, no ears at all!) in all the record companies, with one exception. New Zealander Chris Parry, who was responsible for signing The Jam, Otway And Barrett and Siouxsie And The Banshees to Polydor Records, heard the tape and was impressed. He was so impressed, in fact, he immediately wrote to Robert and asked to meet with the band.

Parry was thinking of leaving Polydor's cushy A&R Department to go it alone with his own label and was determined to make The Cure his first signing. Whilst the band were disappointed that they were not being picked up by a major, they immediately warmed to Parry and, two meetings later, they signed an initial six-month contract with the newly formed Fiction Records. Michael Dempsey commented in 'Ten Imaginary Years': "He never explained what he saw in us. We were a three-piece, The Jam were a three-piece and I got the feeling that maybe he thought 'I'll go for another one' - not consciously but like when you need a pair of shoes and there's a tendency to go and buy a similar pair to the ones you're used to."

Whatever Parry saw in them, he had a great deal riding on that particular signing. To break away from the relative financial security of a major record company with all its resources takes nerve and, although Fiction was primarily funded by Polydor, Parry's reputation was on the line. His first signing HAD to be a success. To achieve this end, Parry acted as their Godfather, handling everything from production and press to humping the band's gear and mixing their live shows. He threw himself into all these jobs whole-heartedly and it is probably not underestimating the band's unique talent to say that without Parry's initial enthusiasm and tireless effort on their behalf, they would not be the success that they are today.

On September 20th, The Cure went into Morgan's Studio 4 to record masters for their debut album, this time with Chris Parry at the production helm. Although the sessions were not conducted entirely without conflict between Parry and Robert, they emerged two days later with five tracks completed: 'Killing An Arab', '10.15', 'Fire In Cairo', 'Plastic Passion' and 'Three Imaginary Boys'. Parry

DOMINION THEATRE
TOTTENHAM COURT ROAD LONDON W1
Derek Block presents
THE CURE
CLASSIX NOUVEAUX
THE VISITORS
MONDAY 17th NOVEMBER 7·30pm

remarked later: "I had a production concept - here was a three piece but, rather than make them sound like a f[...] piece like I did The Jam, I wanted to make it totally different, elusive, translucent, stripped right down to the bones. I liked the lyrics and I liked Robert's voice and I was convinced, after the punk thrash, that peop[...] would want something more mysterious."

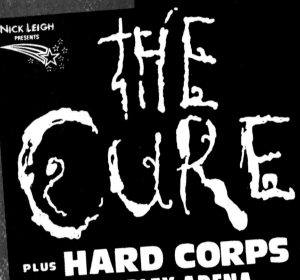

After the recording sessions, Parry booke[...] them a series of dates specifically so they could gain experience playing live and develop their stagecraft techniques. He also began w[...] on their nonexistent image, without much success. Although Michael and Lol attempted to give some thought to the way they looke[...] on stage, Robert would have none of it, seeming distinctly uncomfortable with the notio[...] of image. His only compromise was by buying himself a pair of new shoes!

For the next two months they began t[...] gig almost every night. One of the mo[...] memorable shows was supporting the UK Subs at the Moonlight Club in We[...] Hampstead on 20th November. It was memorable because Robert insisted o[...] cuttingly rebuffing the Subs' vocalist, Charlie Harper. The UK Subs were n[...] spring chickens and Robert felt the punk movement was about youth. Consequently, they were not amongs[...] Robert's favourite punk bands and he told Harper so. After a heated discussion, The Cure went on to play an extremely aggressive set.

They then embarked on a string of dates supporting Generation X and, in true rock 'n' roll style, paid their dues by driving to and from every show and sleeping on Chris Parry's floor. On 30th November, they played Hales Owen Tiffany's supporting Generation X as a show-case for Polydor executives. Because of this, they were given a hotel room for the night, something which gave the band cause for great excitement at the time. Little did they know then that spending time in hotels would become a rather tedious way of life for them. Nevertheless, this was their first stay in a top rate hotel and they proceeded to celebrate the occasion by getting extremely drunk with the compliments of Polydor Records.

On 5th December, the band played the California Ballroom in Dunstable, their last gig supporting Generation X. Although the headliners continued to tour until the end of the month, The Cure were relieved of their duties as the support act. Rumours abounded that Generation X were not happy by the reaction that their support band were getting from the audience. Indeed, The Cure had improved tremendously during this bout of gigging and, as well as building up a grass-roots following, their sound had become competent, tight and effervescent and the audiences were loving it.

Although this does sound the most likely explanation for the rather unceremonious way in which their tour was cut short, there was also another story circulating. Lol explained: "After the gig, I wandered back through Gen X's dressing room to go to the toilet but someone on the door said I couldn't go in there. Well, I was desperate so I pushed past and went in, and there was Billy Idol up against the urinal in a rather compromising position with a young lady. He gave me his famous sneer but I thought 'Sod it, I'm not going away.' So I walked right up next to him and pulled out my willy and pissed all over him." Fact or fiction, who knows or cares? It makes for a good story and falsification of the truth and manipulating the press was a talent which The Cure were to hone to a fine art over the coming years.

DEREK BLOCK PRESENTS

THE CURE
THE PASSIONS
SECTION 25
PLUS SPECIAL GUESTS
Sunday, May 11th, at 7.30pm
Rainbow Theatre, 232 Seven Sisters Road, London N4
Tickets: £2.75, £2.25, £1.75
Available from Rainbow 01-263 3148/9 and usual agents

December also saw their debut Radio One session. They performed 'Killing An Arab', '10.15 Saturday Night', 'Fire In Cairo' and 'Boys Don't Cry' for John Peel's late night show. This was to be the first of many radio sessions.

Another first was the appearance of a feature in the New Musical Express by Adrian Thrills entitled 'Ain't No Blues For The Summertime Cure'. Chris Parry had driven Thrills to one of the band's earlier gigs but he had made no real comment that he had liked the band. Parry had thought Thrills would have been bowled over by them, as

SIGN

NAMES AND PLACES. AND WARNINGS...

indeed he had been, but when he didn't voice his opinions, Parry felt that he had made a mistake in taking him to see the band. When the article came out, Parry was ecstatic. Thrills wrote a rave review calling the band "a breath of fresh suburban air in the capital's smog-ridden pub circuit." He urged people to catch The Cure's live performance immediately and, such is the power of the press, that is exactly what they did. When they played the Hope & Anchor in London's Islington on December 19th, the venue was packed with curious punters and members of the music press. Parry's gamble had paid off and, although Robert had flu and Lol's drumkit kept falling over, they were reviewed favourably.

Rick Joseph wrote: "A youthful nervousness, dotted with moments of controlled deadpan enhanced their stage presence; they played with sufficient enthusiasm to overcome the Spartan test-tube conditions of this chilly niterie. Hollering for two encores, the crowd risked frostbite to clap for The Cure."

Whilst the band was busy making a lasting impression on audiences around London, Parry was hard at work scheduling the release of their first single.

Because of Fiction's association with Polydor, all product was to be manufactured and distributed by the major record company. However, it was just before Christmas and it is notoriously difficult for a major label to successfully market anything but established acts during the flurry of releases at this time. The lead up to Yuletide is the busiest time of the year and the record companies

THE CURE: 'Killing An Arab' *****
Strange single, from this rapidly rising three-
piece. Eerie music, nasaled, tired vocals. Sounds
like a single of the year to me. Watch this space
for further scam on these young gentlemen. A
goodie.

simply don't have the time or resources
necessary to break an unknown act. In
fact, some would call it commercial
suicide to attempt such a release but
not, it seems, Chris Parry.

Having worked at Polydor for
many years, he was well aware
of its weaknesses and decided,
instead, to put out 'Killing An
Arab'/'10.15 Saturday Night' by way of
a one-off single deal on Small Wonder,
an independent label operating from a
record store in Walthamstow. Small
Wonder had the facilities to press
15,000 copies and, if the single sold
well, Fiction would have made money
to press a further 15,000 themselves.

The Cure's debut single was released
on 22nd December 1978, accompanied
by a poster campaign of dubious
design portraying an old man's face,
reversed out to make it look more ugly.

THE CURE: "Killing An Arab" (Small Wonder II). Apres La Chute, Le Deluge . . . Camus' The Outsider condensed into a sparse, monotone 45 which, after a marvellous descending guitar figure, manages to slip past with less impact than expected. Maybe that's part of the point: like novel, like record. Another illustration of the (often disturbing) melting-pot that pop has become: another book, another image or selling point — meanwhile the past is neatly plundered, rewritten and re-assembled to be bought and danced to. It has to be said in this case, however, that the Cure . . . with commendable understatement . . .

Parry remarked later: "The design certainly wasn't to Robert's taste, I knew that, but I wasn't terribly concerned. I just wanted him to concentrate on the music." In January the glowing reviews of the single that appeared in the music press revealed that Parry's strategy had paid off. Again.

Dave McCullouch wrote in Sounds: "'Killing An Arab' is unfair in a way as a record. O.K., the, Ah, 'A' side (well, the side that gives you the impression of being the 'A' side) is nice and fresh and crisp and funny. Quaint. You immediately LOVE it. But it's the reverse side, entitled rather magnificently '10.15', that stops you right in your tracks as you walk lifelessly back from the dust covered record deck.

"Music this good and original is always

WORD

UP

done a grave disservice by being gauchely filtered through the medium of words. Words, moreover, that are being hurriedly and excitedly hammered out by an over impetuous, over rushed CHILD of a writer.

"'10.15' hits upon the value of sparseness in rock 'n' roll like no other record has in, oh, as far as I can think back. There's scarcely any playing on the song at all! Imagine feeling recharged on a Monday morning. I suppose I was even whistling a pleasant air as I dive-bombed for my trusty phone book that was to lead me on the trail of this band, this medicine, this, ahem, Cure. Go."

Inevitably, 'Killing An Arab' elicited misguided charges of racism although the band were quick to explain that the song was inspired by 'The Stranger', a novel by the French writer Albert Camus. During a gig at London's Nashville the following month, the National Front actually turned up and disrupted the show with continuous fighting because they took the title of the song literally and began distributing leaflets on the subject.

The band had no option but to immediately publish denials and had to play the single down to diffuse an unpleasant situation which could have been extremely damaging to their career.

On 8th January, The Cure went back into Morgan studios to complete their debut album with Parry producing and aided by an engineer called Hedges. They laid the tracks down in record time, sometimes in only three or four takes and the sound was enhanced by a newly acquired Fender Jazzmaster

guitar and a Roland JC 160 amp.

The Cure had greatly impressed
Sounds' writer Dave McCullouch,
normally a very hard man to please. He
had requested an interview which had
taken place at the Natural History
Museum and, on January 27th, the
interview was published accompanied
by a front cover. Now, front covers are
not particularly easy to come by and
are the subject of fierce competition, so
to have been awarded such an
accolade so early in their career was
quite an achievement. This cover,
along with the reviews of the single lit
the fuse for much media scrutiny and
the music press moved in speedily -
almost overnight.

he NME's Nick Kent wrote with
prophetic accuracy: "The Cure
are brighter than the usual
middle-class suburbanites, as self-
protective as they are self-effacing.
They are not rude, or particularly
cliquish but the interviewer senses that
the ongoing interview situation is not
one that they feel particularly at home
with, that they find the process
bemusing, almost quaint, in its
ridiculousness. As personalities,
drummer Tolhurst appears the most
democratic and business-like, while
guitarist Smith, definitely 'older' than his
age is the creative shoulder-shrugging
one, replete with a brand of cynicism
that hides the plethora of changes his
personality and current context will later
lead him to refer to. Between this pair,
bassist Dempsey blends in without
adding any particular
dimension.....What will follow may
well be some of the finest pop of the
80's. The Cure and Smith in
particular are to be watched closely."

In between giving interviews to an

insatiable media and mixing their album, they emerged now and then to play live dates. At one of these gigs, The Moonlight Club in West Hampstead, the music press turned out in force. Nick Kent, again: "Each and every song struck no pose but delivered an intriguing hook-line here, and obvious sturdy substance there. The material at first hearing ranged from excellent pop (primarily what could be their next single, the irresistible 'Boys Don't Cry') to invigorating, well-structured rock."

From 4th March The Cure played a residency of four sell-out Sunday nights at London's famous Marquee Club, supported on one occasion by Joy Division and on another by Fashion. Reviewing one of the gigs, James Truman wrote "In the final count, The Cure are doing what few of the other new bands have done, writing traditionally melodic songs, embracing experiment to a point short of self-indulgence and, at the same time, being intelligent about it. They are very young. They will also be successful." As far as the majority of the press were concerned, they could do no wrong.

more live dates followed, at several of which strange events occurred. At a gig at Bournemouth Town Hall, a girl reportedly pulled her boyfriend's ear off (HOW she pulled it off remains a mystery to this day) the deed lending itself nicely for some national press exposure and, on 8th March at Hounslow Borough College, there was an ugly scene between the security (all

QUALITY

TOLERANCE, HUMOUR, INTELLIGENCE, SILENCE WANTING TO KNOW

off-duty firemen) and a large number of
skinheads who objected to the reggae
support band. Both situations raised
the band's public profile nicely.

The album was now complete,
leaving only the artwork to be
designed, the very same
artwork which was to baffle the critics
on the album's release. Parry
explained: "My problem with The Cure
was, here was a band without an image
but with strong music so I thought 'Let's
make it completely without an image'
rather than go for the sort of blood,
gore and angst display that was
popular for album covers at the time.

"I thought, 'let's make it completely
dispassionate, let's pick the three most
mundane things we can possibly find'.
And, rather than giving song titles, we
gave clues - the whole thing was a
headache for programmers but it was
an interesting angle. People might be
upset and think it pretentious but that
was a risk I was prepared to take."

The artwork for the album
emerged, depicting a Hoover, a
lampstand and a fridge, all
arranged mundanely on a pink cover.
When Robert saw it for the first time he
was appalled and furious that he hadn't
been consulted on the matter.
However, the deed was done and, on
June 9th 1979, the album entitled
'Three Imaginary Boys' was released
and included the tracks: '10.15
Saturday Night', 'Accuracy', 'Grinding
Halt', 'Another Day', 'Object', 'Subway
Song', 'Foxy Lady', 'Meathook', So
What', 'Fire In Cairo', 'It's Not You' and
'Three Imaginary Boys'. All of the
tracks had been included in their live
set for some time, consequently the
album held few surprises for the music
press.

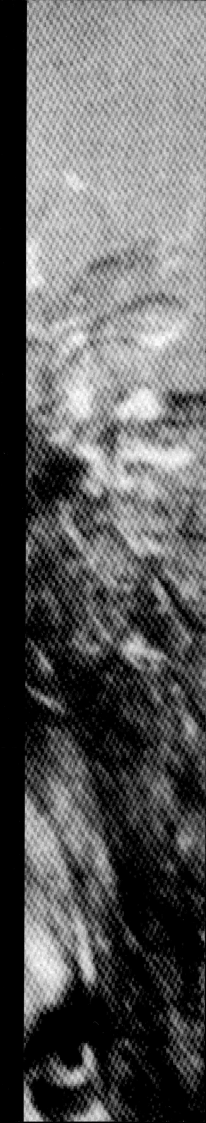

The majority of the reviews, however, were glowing.

Dave McCullough wrote: "The album reflects The Cure's excitement of ideas, their quite stunning sense of the reserved, the sparse, the low-key: they achieve what others employ battalions on with the simple unit of bass, guitar, drums and voice. Satire? The gross becomes the intense. The chic becomes the workable."

elody Maker's Ian Birch agreed: "Their songs run through a whole gamut of moods which grow out of everyday situations: anger, mischief, disillusion, scorn, wistfulness and humour. Their appeal is immediate but still has the kind of depth that allow them to resonate in your head a long time afterwards. They're tightly structured, but also open-ended enough to be accessible to everyone. They are astute without being condescending, provocative without losing sight of that basic aim of entertainment."

High praise indeed. However, despite these glowing press reviews, the album only reached No.44 in the UK charts.

The Cure had embarked on a UK tour some months earlier and several of the shows were marred by various incidents. On 5th April they played Chesterton Fusion Hall, the first gig there since Pink Floyd played in 1968. At the hotel after the concert, the police raided the rooms, being used by the band and crew, for drugs. The band's rooms were clean, but a quantity of an illegal substance was found upon the person of one of the roadies. The poor

"YES OR NO"
A PHRASE I OFTEN TACK ONTO THE END OF A FOOLISH QUESTION WHEN ATTEMPTING TO ELICIT A QUICK RESPONSE FROM SOME-ONE NEAR ME.

unfortunate was arrested and later appeared in court for possession.

The following day, they played Watford College and it was at the gig that the local skinheads chose to do battle with the police and a pack of police dogs. However, the best was yet to come.

On 29th April at the Northgate Community Centre in their home town of Crawley, they played a benefit performance for Dr. Weaver, an old school teacher friend of both Robert and Lol, who had lost several teaching jobs due to his homosexuality. Robert takes up the story: "The National Front turned up again and went berserk. They ringed the community centre and tried to burn it down while we were playing. The whole night was a disaster really, pure violence from beginning to end, as all the Anti Nazi League people turned up as well. It was a shambles, but it made the papers..." Certainly, it would be suffice to say that, since inception, incidents which seem to happen to or around The Cure never leave the media short of good copy.

The majority of the music papers had run features on the band by this time. It seemed that everybody had to have their dose of The Cure. Striking while the iron was hot, Parry sent out white labels of 'Grinding Halt' to the press and radio stations, with a view to releasing the track as a second single. The response was poor so, in late June, 'Boys Don't Cry'/'Plastic Passion' was released instead. The 'A' side was a firm favourite with the press who had seen it performed live and, like its predecessor, gave it rave reviews. However, despite having everything in its favour, the single failed to chart. The band and Parry, who was

"POSITIVELY THE LAST VERSE OF 'A FOREST" VOWS ROBERT Smith!
EXCLUSIVE

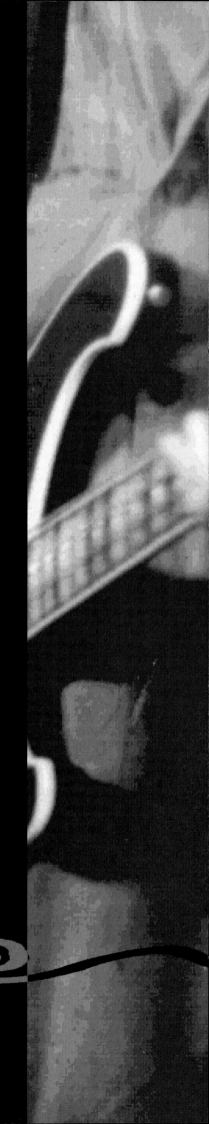

convinced along with the rest of the world that the single was a hit, were incredibly disappointed, resulting in Parry acrimoniously claiming they had been "stitched up" by Polydor.

ndeterred, the band continued with their tour and, on 1st July, they headlined The Lyceum, supported by The Ruts. On 29th July, they played their first foreign gig, an outdoor festival in Sterrebos, Holland. They went down very well with the Dutch audience but were less than impressed with the accommodation that had been provided - a dirty, smelly room on the tenth floor of a seedy hotel in Amsterdam, furnished with six camp beds. Although, at that time, they shunned the unadulterated luxury enjoyed by successful rock bands, even they must have felt that this was taking things a little too far. However, they returned to Britain none the worse for their experience in time for a fortuitous meeting which was to set the scene for the next five or six years.

On 3rd August Robert met Steve Severin of The Banshees at a Throbbing Gristle show at the YMCA in London's Tottenham Court Road. Robert struck an amusing figure in a lurid green check Charlie Cairoli suit and sunglasses which greatly amused Severin. The two immediately found they had mutual interests, including Parry, who had been responsible for signing both bands, and got on famously. So famously, in fact, that by the end of the evening Robert had agreed that The Cure would support The Banshees on their forthcoming tour.

On August 24th, The Cure played the first night of the annual Reading Festival on a bill with The Tourists, The

PARADISE

A COLD GLASS OF WATER IN THE DESERT

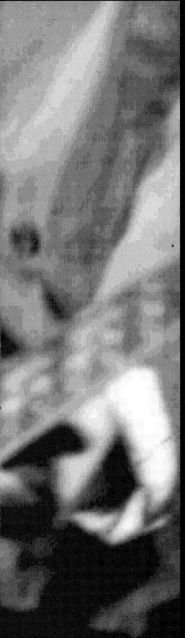

Police, Motorhead, Wilko Johnson and Doll By Doll. They shared a caravan with Motorhead and were mightily impressed with the impressive Lemmy. They even dedicated 'Boys Don't Cry' to him - very apt in Lemmy's case - and were extremely well received by the audience.

n 5th September, they played the Ulster Hall in Belfast - their first gig supporting Siouxsie and The Banshees. Although the band had arrived in Northern Ireland with plenty of time to spare, it soon became evident that their equipment hadn't. It was, in fact, still in Liverpool - courtesy of the crew who had fallen asleep and missed the ferry. The Cure finally borrowed enough gear to go on stage but not in time for the support slot. The Banshees had to appear first and The Cure played a dazzling set in the headline slot, managing to lose one of the guitars borrowed from The Outcasts as they did so. Quite some start!

The next day, The Cure travelled to

Unfortunately, Polydor had only delivered 50 of the 200 albums that the store had ordered and these had sold out within minutes, a situation which enraged both the fans and the band. However, whilst the Banshees' manager tried to pour oil on troubled water by selling the shop a supply from the back of his car, guitarist John McKay and drummer Kenny Morris had a blazing argument with the other band members, stormed out of the shop and, stopping at the hotel only to collect their belongings and pin their tour passes to their pillows, caught the first train back to London.

This display of extremely unprofessional behaviour wasn't discovered until The Banshees' entourage were leaving the hotel to travel to the venue, at approximately the same time that The Cure were going on stage. Backstage, during The Cure's set, all hell had broken loose and they were requested to keep on playing while the headliners' management and promoters racked their brains for a solution. Eventually, Steve Severin and Siouxsie went on stage and explained the situation to the crowd which was greeted by much disappointed chanting. Finally, The Cure went back on stage and performed some new songs which were still awaiting lyrics, with the show ending when they were joined by Severin and Siouxsie for a rendition of The Banshees' 'The Lord's Prayer'.

Robert explained later: "Severin was shouting to me 'E! Just play E!' and, as it turned out, that wasn't to be the last time he shouted it at me either!"

Derek Block presents

THE CURE

plus GUESTS

26th NOV. EDINBURGH ODEON
27th NOV. GLASGOW PAVILION
28th NOV. BRADFORD ST.GEORGES HALL
29th NOV. STOKE KINGS HALL
30th NOV. COVENTRY APOLLO
3rd DEC. HAMMERSMITH PALAIS

All tickets £3.50 & £3.00 except
Hammersmith Palais, all £3.50

Back at The Banshees' hotel later that night, Robert, Siouxsie and Steve Severin talked until the early hours of the morning over more than a few drinks. During these discussions, Robert volunteered his services on guitar, should they be required. Although Robert probably thought that this was just another drunken conversation in another hotel bar, the pair duly noted his offer. However, the dates at Glasgow Apollo, Dunfermline Kinnema, St. Georges Hall in Bradford and Oxford New Theatre were cancelled in order to allow The Banshees time to sort out their personnel problems and they began the laborious task of auditioning drummers and guitarists, hundreds of whom had answered an appeal broadcast on the John Peel Show.

During this unexpected break in the tour, The Cure kept busy. On 10 September they played the Rotterdam New Pop Festival in front of an audience of 10,000. The show was also filmed for Dutch television and broadcast nationally. On their return to Britain, they went back into Morgan and began work on their next single, 'Jumping Someone Else's Train'/'I'm Cold'.

It was during these sessions that Michael became unhappy with the direction in which The Cure was heading. He didn't like the two new tracks and liked the fact that the basslines were being simplified even less. However, he was unable to argue his point due to Robert insisting that he record his guitar parts and vocals separately. There is nothing particularly unusual about a band laying down their respective parts without all the band members being present but it had never happened in The Cure before

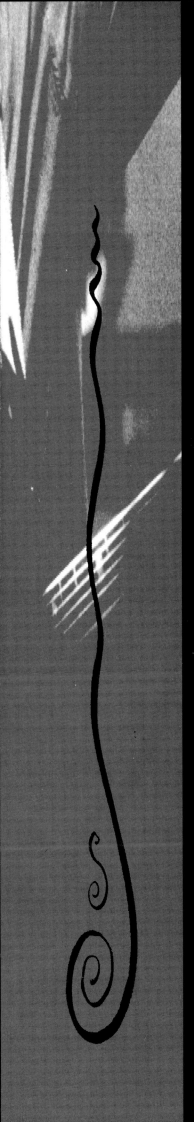

and Michael became suspicious of Robert's motives although he kept his resentment close to his chest.

During Robert's time in the studio, he was joined by the two remaining Banshees, with Siouxsie contributing the backing vocals to 'I'm Cold'. However, the pair had ulterior motives for joining Robert at the studio. Although they had auditioned literally dozens of musicians for the vacancies arising from the departure of Morris and McKay, they had not found a suitable replacement guitarist. Ex-Slits drummer Budgie had been recruited as the new drummer and they had thought further about Robert's offer of help and decided that he would be just right to complete the line-up. They offered him the job during the sessions and Robert agreed on the condition that The Cure remain the support act. This meant that Robert would have to play two different sets every night, a feat requiring a huge amount of energy.

Robert recalled: "I don't remember it being difficult. After what we'd been doing for the past two or three years, it was a piece of piss really. We were driven around, there was food in the dressing room and the only difficult thing was the mental strain of the first few nights because I knew people were looking at me, thinking 'Is he going to be able to do this?'

"I got through it okay, though it was the first time I'd ever tried to copy a guitarist. I found that peculiar, but more rewarding than exhausting."

The Banshees' tour resumed, with Robert playing his duel roles, on 18th September at the De Montford Hall in Leicester. The NME wrote: "Smith has a task which would have daunted lesser players; after first coming on with his own lot, he's gotta abruptly change guitar and mood to play an unfamiliar act. But he handles this enforced schizophrenia with the minimum of fuss, and armed with a new guitar and flanger (to get that swishing McKay tone) comes out on top, cautious but convincing."

The tour continued in this fashion. Michael became even more despondent as the spotlight began firmly focusing on Robert and felt that his sudden celebrity was overshadowing and damaging The Cure as a whole. He also disapproved of Robert spending most of his time in the Banshee camp, both out of choice and necessity.

The Banshees had a luxury tour bus and felt that Robert should travel with them in order to avoid arriving at the various gigs at different times. However, while Robert travelled in the lap of luxury, Lol and Michael slogged up and down motorways in an old green Maxi like second-class citizens. It is easy to see why the whole state of affairs had become a breeding ground for resentment and contempt. Lol, however, seemed to be oblivious to the situation. He got on well with Steve Severin and the rest of The Banshees and was enjoying touring with them.

The tour came to a close on 15th October at London's Hammersmith Odeon and Michael Dempsey quit the band, not entirely unexpectedly. He told the NME: "I suppose you could call it a clash of personalities, but I was

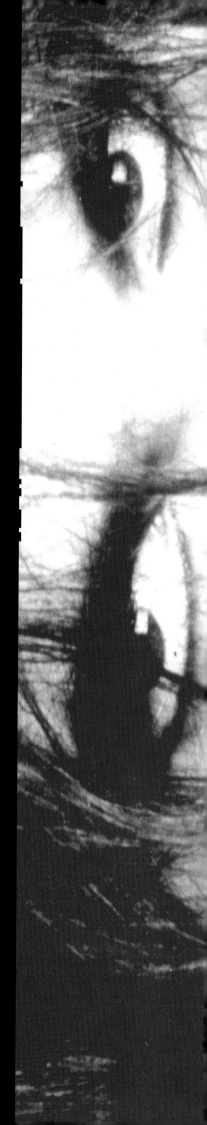

definitely booted out and I'm looking for
another gig." He eventually found one
with labelmates, The Associates.

obert told the NME some eight
months later: I'd known Lol
since I was six, but not
Michael. The differences were between
him and me. The more it went on, the
more unbearable it became. I found on
The Banshees' tour that I was enjoying
playing with The Banshees more than I
was with The Cure. That's what really
made the decision. Lol felt the same
way. Michael wasn't criticising or
joining in on any level. We were getting
sort of banal. We were sticking to the
same set night after night and the
whole thing was getting like a joke.
None of us were enjoying it, there
wasn't much point in carrying on."

During November, Fiction released
'Jumping Someone Else's Train'/'I'm
Cold' but, again despite critical acclaim,
it failed to chart.

With the strain of the Banshees tour
behind him, Robert spent time on his
own in Crawley, experimenting with
different sounds. Using his sister's
Hammond organ which was fully
equipped with bass pedals and drum
machine, he soon began to get ideas
down on tape, building up half a dozen
songs within a week. The songs were
received by an enthusiastic Lol and
Robert also played them to old mate
and bass player, Simon Gallup with a
view to him filling the vacancy caused
by Michael Dempsey's departure.

Simon said later in 'Ten Imaginary
Years': "I always felt I ought to be their
bass player but I never dreamed
Robert would ask me. I was resigned to
spending my life working in the factory
from 7.30 to 5.30, coming home,

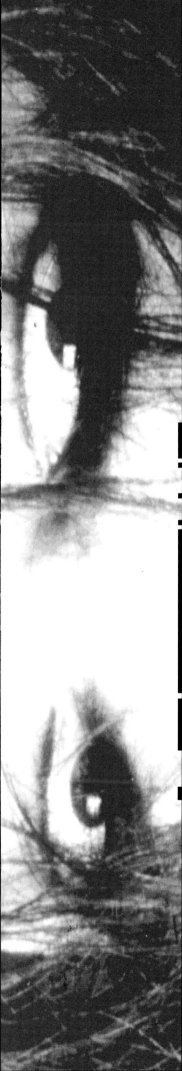

playing bass for a couple of hours, spending the rest of the evening with Carol, my girlfriend, and then, at the end of the week, going down the pub with my eighteen quid."

The Cure were back to being a trio again but Robert had ideas to take the band one step further and recruited keyboard player Matthieu Hartley, the proud owner of a Korg Duophonic synth. The four-piece immediately began rehearsing at Robert's house, inviting Chris Parry down to sample their wares. Chris was less than enthusiastic with the set up and felt that Robert had been rather over-zealous by recruiting two new band members. He also took an instant dislike to Matthieu, finding him overbearing and boorish. On a more positive note, he liked Simon enormously and, when they started playing, he was impressed. The sound was certainly different from anything that had gone before but it was no less valid.

The new-look Cure made its debut at Eric's in Liverpool as part of The Future Pastimes Tour, a package of Fiction acts including The Passions and The Associates. Needless to say, it was eventful.

Their tour bus broke down en route to the gig and they didn't arrive at the venue until 10.00 pm, by which time The Passions had already played and there were only about one hundred people in the audience. Robert had been drinking on the trip from London and was reasonably mellow by the time they reached their destination. After a couple of beers in the bar, he was relaxed enough to saunter on stage and play what would be best described

NUMBER

THREE

as a band rehearsal. Robert chatted between songs and to the audience - which comprised of a lot of their fans from Sussex - forgot the lyrics and concluded their performance by throwing up over a punk in the first row! A good night was obviously had by all.

obert told Record Mirror: "We were actually beginning to feel like a group. If you're in a band and you're playing together for a concentrated period of time you have to get on with each other - unless you're only in it for the money, which we're not. It's not so much the unity of thinking, because everybody thinks differently, but the unity of ideas. If someone thinks something they say it. And despite what the press think there's no hierarchy in The Cure. If there's one drink on the table we all fight for it."

The Future Pastimes Tour slowly made its way around the university circuit ending at Crawley College, The Cure's home town, on 7th December. The inevitable skinheads began bottling each other at the gig which was a sad note on which to have ended as a lot of family and friends had turned out to see them.

Following the end of the tour, The Cure headed for Europe for an eleven-date tour including shows in Eindhoven, Amsterdam and Paris. They were well received everywhere.

On January 3rd 1980, the band began rehearsing for their next album and, on 13th January, they went back into Morgan to commence recording. This time, however, Robert had very definite ideas of his own as to how the band should be produced and requested that Chris Parry did not attend the sessions.

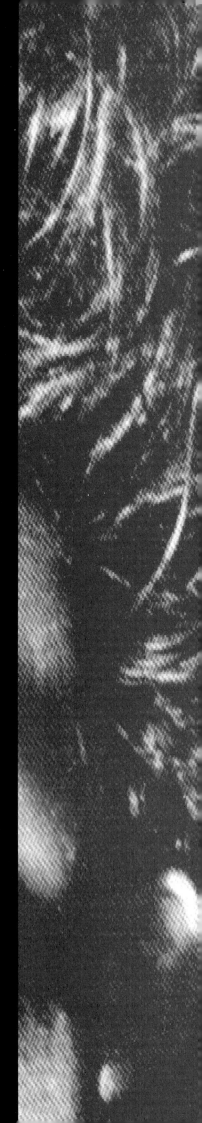

He wanted to produce the album himself along with the help of engineer Mike Hedges. Many of the songs' arrangements had already been worked out by playing them live on the previous tour and the sessions went very well, especially so as neither Simon nor Matthieu had ever worked in a studio before.

Parry, who was expecting a disaster, was pleasantly surprised when he finally got to hear the unmixed tracks. He said: "I was called over to hear 'A Forest' and it was wonderful. The whole album had been done very economically which was great. They worked all the hours of the day, went to bed at four in the morning, the bloody hoover came in at ten or whatever and woke them up a bit grumpy, but they were young enough to take it and that created a kind of mystique."

ll the tracks were mixed in six days and, on 10th February, they had completed the album entitled 'Seventeen Seconds'. Tracks included were: 'A Reflection', 'Play For Today', 'Secrets', 'In Your House', 'Three', 'The Final Sound', 'A Forest', 'M', 'At Night' and 'Seventeen Seconds'.

Free from the restraints of the studio, The Cure played The Lakeside in Crawley, joined by Porl Thompson for an encore of a song entitled 'I'm A Cult Hero'. The previous October, Fiction had released a single of the same name by Cult Hero - in reality The Cure. It was a spoof song, sardonically ridiculing their own situation. Although it didn't make the charts in the UK, it did go on to sell over 35,000 copies in Canada. On 23rd March, The Cult Heroes played their one and only gig, supporting The Passions at London's Marquee Club after one day's rehearsal. The band comprised of a postman called Frank Bell providing the vocals, two schoolgirl backing vocalists and the four Cure band members. They played various early Seventies tunes including 'Do You Wanna Touch' by Gary Glitter, 'Whiskey In The Jar' by Thin Lizzy and Sweet's 'Blockbuster'. The alcohol flowed, the faithful from Crawley arrived to sing along and the whole gig was taken in the humour in which it was intended providing some much needed light relief.

In April, Robert contributed backing vocals for The Associates forthcoming album and made a guest appearance on guitar with The Stranglers at London's Rainbow

63

Theatre. Hugh Cornwall, The Strangler's vocalist, had recently been imprisoned on a drugs charge and an all-star line-up had been assembled to play as a protest.

On 5th April 'A Forest'/'Another Journey By Train' was released as a single and, at last, won the band some chart success by finally peaking at No. 31. in May.

On 10th April, The Cure crossed the Atlantic to play in America for the first time. It was a short tour and done on a low budget, but the band was well received, although they had only attained cult status there. They played one night in Philadelphia, Washington and Boston but sold out three nights at Hurrah in New York. Sounds journalist Phil Sutcliffe accompanied them and had witnessed Robert's abhorrence of the whole rock 'n' roll trip which prevails in the States.

Derek Block presents

THE CURE
PLUS GUESTS

TUES 20th APRIL
BRISTOL COLSTON HALL
ALL TICKETS £3.50

WED 21st APRIL
BRIGHTON DOME
ALL TICKETS £3.50

THURS 22nd APRIL
SOUTHAMPTON GAUMONT
TICKETS £3.50 £3.25

SAT 24th APRIL
NEWCASTLE CITY HALL
TICKETS £3.50 £3.25

SUN 25th APRIL
GLASGOW PAVILION
TICKETS £3.75 £3.25

MON 26th APRIL
EDINBURGH PLAYHOUSE
TICKETS £3.75 £3.50 £3.25

TUES 27th APRIL
MANCHESTER APOLLO
TICKETS £3.50 £3.25

WED 28th APRIL
BIRMINGHAM ODEON
TICKETS £3.50 £3.25

SAT 1st MAY
HAMMERSMITH ODEON
TICKETS £4.00 & £3.50

TICKETS ON SALE NOW CHECK BOX OFFICES FOR DETAILS

The Cure's American record company tried to heighten the band's profile by arranging an impromptu photosession with Debbie Harry backstage after one of their gigs at Hurrah. He wrote: "Robert Smith hadn't been very nice about it all, I gathered. While the star smiled her smile and joked about 'Hey, your credibility's gone now' the artist turned his back to the camera and tried to screw all the photographer's attempts to get a shot for the biz magazines like Cashbox and Billboard who run lots of snaps of people shaking hands so that the corporate readers can see everybody's happy and everything's right in this best of all megaprofitable worlds.

Whereas Robert Smith doesn't believe it and would rather not endorse it or supply their need for reassurance."

Matthieu revealed to Phil Sutcliffe various games the band had devised to keep boredom at bay during the long and tedious journeys on the road. One was imagining the perfect place for each of them to live :"Mine would be a vegetable garden I could eat my way through forever. Simon's town had everything made of leather, even the houses, and inflatable wimps you could chain to your leg and kick as you went along. Tolhurstville was a long street with a sweet shop then a pub then a toilet, then the same again and again into infinity. Robert's place would be full of people in separate rooms sitting and staring at the walls."

After their gig in Boston the band, along with Parry, drove back to New York in record time to try to catch a flight back to Britain as The Cure had been invited to appear on Top Of The Pops due to the success of 'A Forest'. They made the flight with only moments to spare and dashed straight to the Top Of The Pops' studio when the plane landed at Heathrow. Suffering from jet-lag, the band made their way to the bar, where they tried to avoid the other bands appearing on the BBC TV show. Robert was also in pain from an injury to his thumb which he had sustained a couple of days earlier whilst trying to change a flat tyre. An

OBJECT

SOMETHING OUT OF CONTEXT LIKE
A SEVERED HAND.
A FIGUREHEAD : THE GLAZE MADE DULL
BY DUST ...

injury to a finger is one of the most debilitating and painful afflictions for a guitarist, and it certainly showed in his performance that day. Robert sported a huge bandage on his thumb which rendered playing guitar impossible and the band looked generally morose and

disinterested, partially because they were exhausted and partially because Robert, in particular didn't approve of the show's poppy image.

He remarked later: "I hated Top Of The Pops because I was getting to this phase where I was really anti everything like that, anti pop. I didn't want The Cure to be a pop band though I was convinced we should do Top Of The Pops because I realised, even then, that, if we didn't do it somebody else would and it made no difference to the majority of the people watching whether we played or not."

Obviously the majority of people watching didn't think much of their dismal display, as the single immediately plunged down the charts!

On 10 May, the album 'Seventeen Seconds' was released. The album cover was, as usual, obscure and depicted photographs of the four band members on the back which were blurred and out of focus. Unlike with 'Three Imaginary Boys', this time Robert had control over the artwork and liked the design, despite protestations from Parry that it was too vague.

The album's content was certainly very different from 'Three Imaginary Boys' and, on the whole, the press weren't as complimentary. Robert gave an insight into his feelings when he told the NME:

"It was a really condensed incident, a rush of feelings that I'd found in myself had been watered down, mainly by playing in a group. It's a really strange situation but I find touring and things like that shut me down. I harden and get very reclusive, sort of shun people. I'm not naturally an extrovert person but sometimes I get really withdrawn and it irritates people. They think I'm doing it on purpose. Sometimes I don't like talking to people, which isn't important, but I don't like people saying 'Oh no, here we go again, he's not being sociable!' and it's just something that happened, all the things that I'd been shutting down just came out in a big rush and, for the following two weeks, every day I'd be thinking about that one particular incident. One day I'd wake up wanting to kill somebody, the next day I wouldn't even bother getting up. It was awful.

"I was letting myself slip in order to write songs. I wasn't fighting it whereas, in everyday life, you'd have to control those feelings. But it's good that it happened. At the time I was shutting down and didn't feel like writing any more songs, I just couldn't be bothered; and it was actually through being in a group! Through actually playing songs! That was causing me to stop writing songs."

 espite what the press thought of the album and regardless of the emotion behind its creation, it reached a very reasonable No. 20 in the UK charts and, on 25th April, The Cure embarked on a British tour concluding on May 11th at London's Rainbow Theatre supported by The

Passions, The Fall and The Au Pairs.

ounds journalist Johnny Waller reviewed their Edinburgh show: "The Cure's show - and a show it most decidedly is, featuring all the singles - is based on an assured control over their instruments, their material and their audience. Vocalist and main-man Robert Smith maintains an unruffled calm, taking everything in his stride as would a man on a Sunday afternoon stroll.

"Gone is a certain amount of the pent-up frustration I witnessed at the claustrophobic gig at Valentino's recently, when The Cure almost personified teenage angst and self-doubt. Perhaps they've matured overnight (or maybe it's just the atmosphere of the seated venue this time) but keyboardist Matthieu Hartley is especially listless, wandering off stage for a cigarette during those songs to which he does not contribute. Only Simon Gallup (on bass, leather jacket and youth rebellion) carries the day convincingly.

"But it's two encores to a capacity audience (with an Afghan coat here and there!) and I'm only quibbling because I know how good the Cure can be. This was not their best, and I hope (for their sakes as well as mine) that it's only a temporary fault. The Cure are too vital to mellow out so young."

The British tour complete, the band embarked on their first full European tour - complete with the inevitable mishaps.

In Holland, the band were arrested for public indecency after a spot of skinnydipping in Rotterdam. Although

the alleged offence occurred in the early hours of the morning and only affronted one old lady unlucky enough to have been looking out of her window, the Dutch police arrived on the scene of the crime en masse, armed and extremely dangerous! After a nasty spell in the back of a police van where their belongings were searched, they were released.

Further disasters occurred including the following: having their truck impounded before boarding the ferry to Sweden, a van breakdown in Belgium, a badly injured roadie in Harrenthout, a PA blow-up in Utrecht when someone poured beer over the amps, a brawl with Brussels barmen (they'd accused the band's sound man of being under age when he was, in fact, thirty-one) which led to producer Mike Hedges going to hospital in need of eighteen stitches and, later, the hospitalisation of their driver due to pulled back muscles! And this was just the tip of the iceberg!

On 14 June, The Cure were scheduled to play a festival in France, headlined by Roxy Music, with UFO, The Clash and Kevin Coyne. There was a riot and the French police used tear-gas to disperse the crowd and which Roxy Music decided not to play. The show ended in complete chaos. However, whilst they were in France they performed one show which was recorded by French radio. One number entitled 'At Night' was later to appear on 'Curiosity'.

They returned to the UK and played three dates in Scotland and, in July, they went back to Holland where their popularity was rapidly increasing and played a series of outdoor festivals.

Their performance at Venedaal was recorded by Dutch radio for broadcast later in the year. At this time, NME journalist Paul Morley interviewed the band and astutely noted of Robert: "He's always on a fine line between agitation and boredom, and such a balance turns out faintly, deviously charming. He's no pretentious mock-recluse, perpetually feigning intensity of vision. He's never quite sure what to say. He's never quite sure of those around him. Does he take himself too seriously?"

During the interview Robert also explained: "I've always written things down, ever since I could remember. Mainly because sometimes I get really angry. I've got a really violent temper but it's not physical because I don't think I should vent my frustrations and depressions onto anyone else. I don't through tantrums or anything like that so I go off somewhere rather than smash the room. I write things down. It's a release."

On 24th July, The Cure left the UK to embark on their first Australasian tour, kicking off in Auckland, New Zealand and quickly moving on to Australia. They were booked to play clubs with tiny stages as the promoters had seriously underestimated their popularity. All the gigs were packed to capacity and, due to the searing heat, the band were dripping with sweat every night. These shows were certainly a far cry from the European festivals to which they had become accustomed. After they had completed the seven shows that had originally been planned, they stayed on in Australia playing more and more gigs due to popular demand, breaking house records wherever they appeared

MUSIC

DREAMS

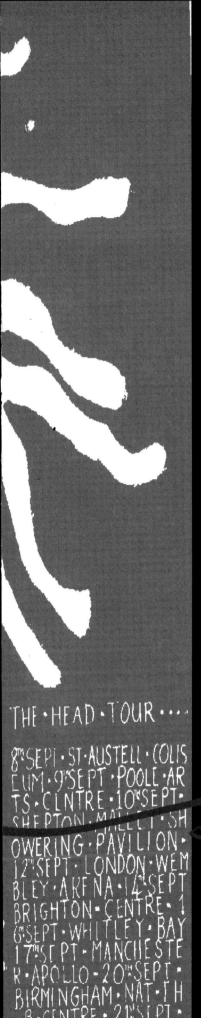

THE·HEAD·TOUR····

8ᵗʰSEPT·ST·AUSTELL·COLIS
EUM·9ᵗʰSEPT·POOLE·AR
TS·CENTRE·10ᵗʰSEPT·
SHEPTON MALLET·SH
OWERING·PAVILION·
12ᵗʰSEPT·LONDON·WEM
BLEY·ARENA·14ᵗʰSEPT
BRIGHTON·CENTRE·1
6ᵗʰSEPT·WHITLEY·BAY
17ᵗʰSEPT·MANCHESTE
R·APOLLO·20ᵗʰSEPT·
BIRMINGHAM·NAT·EH
IB·CENTRE·21ˢᵗSEPT·
LEEDS·QUEENS·HALL
22ⁿᵈSEPT·EDINBURGH
PLAYHOUSE

and taking Australia by storm.

During this tour, the schedule was gruelling, the band lived in close proximity and there were hardly any free days when the band members could take time out from each other. Despite these problems, they were conquering Australia which should have been cause for celebration but, for Matthieu, the strain of the tour was taking its toll and he became increasingly sullen and withdrawn. In addition, he was not happy with the musical direction that the band was taking which was not his style of music at all. He also felt that he was being ostracised by Robert and made up his mind to quit the band.

By the time The Cure had reached Perth and the end of the tour, Robert, Simon and Lol had come to the same conclusion. A few days after they arrived back in the UK, Matthieu called Robert on the telephone and informed him of his decision, much to Robert's relief.

The Cure were a three-piece once more and Robert told Sounds: "It just means that I have to do a bit more work now the keyboards are gone, make more noise. I used to be able to get away with being a lazy sod on stage before."

During October, The Cure completed a further tour of Europe, playing twenty-seven dates and taking in Scandinavia, Holland, Belgium, France and Germany. All the shows were sold-out and 'Seventeen Seconds' reached the Top Ten in both Belgium and Holland. In November, they played university dates in the UK supported by a different band every night - a novel idea of Robert's. They were also

including new songs in their set and working on the arrangements to test their suitability as album tracks.

On 2nd February 1981, the Cure returned to Morgan studios to begin recording their third and most tortuous album, 'Faith'. These sessions were the most difficult of any to that date and the band moved from Morgan to Red Bus studios, then to The Roundhouse, then to Trident and finally to Abbey Road in order to capture the intense, atmospheric, sombre sound that Robert was seeking. His mood at the time was dark, ethereal and depressed due to discussions sparked by the imminent death of Lol's mother and it was this mood he wanted to emulate on the album. He found it almost impossible to achieve.

Robert said later: "The problem was, I was in the right mood when I was on my own with the words and the music but, when I was with the others, it was wrong. It was too happy."

Everyone involved in the production of 'Faith' found it to be a terrible strain. Chris Parry was in despair due to, amongst other factors, the budget being constantly extended and Hedges felt he had reached the upper limit of his working relationship with Robert. Robert, himself, felt that whenever he started to sing the atmosphere would darken. A real sense of relief was felt by all when the album was finally completed. The album included the tracks: 'The Holy Hour', 'Primary', 'Other Voices', 'All Cats Are Grey', 'The Funeral Party', 'Doubt', 'The Drowning Man' and 'Faith'.

After the completion of 'Faith', The Cure composed a sound-track to a short film entitled 'Carnage Visors'

MISERY

FUTILITY

made by Simon's brother Ric, to be shown on their forthcoming British tour instead of a support band. The quality of the film was dubious, due to Ric's inexperience, but, with the tour fast approaching, the band recorded the sound-track at Pont Studios in one day after just three days' rehearsal. The NME reported: "It's not very good, just a series of evolving shapes for people to look at while Smith's austere sound-track further imposes the correct conditions of The Cure's entrance."

On 28th March, the first single from 'Faith' was released entitled 'Primary'/'Descent' and The Cure were invited to perform the track on Top Of The Pops. The band, who still felt the show was crass and tasteless, avoided the other bands as they had before but, this time, swathed their instruments in clothing as a protest against miming. As before, their single, which was at No. 38 plummeted down the charts.

On 11th April, 'Faith' was released, its cover mistily depicting Bolton Abbey in North Yorkshire. It received mixed reviews. Melody Maker's Adam Sweeting wrote: "But it's impressive. The professional genre detective, confronted with the evidence of The Cure's first two albums might have spotted the penchant for pop on the first and detected the spots of blood on the sombre sleeves of the second and added them together. But he couldn't have predicted the richness and deceptive power of 'Faith'."

Record Mirror's Mike Nicholls, never a Cure fan at the best of times wrote: "Whereas PiL, for example, continue to radically rewrite their rule book, The Cure remain stuck in the hackneyed doom-mongering that should have died with Joy Division." Strong stuff!

Despite the uncomplimentary reviews the album went into the UK album charts and peaked at No.14.

obert, by way of an explanation said later in Record Mirror: "It was originally intended to be a very positive record. It turned into a very morbid record. There were just personal reasons which affected everyone at the time. We then had to live with it for a year, in that we toured with it - and it was the one record we shouldn't have done that with, because for one year we lived with this doomy, semi-religious record. We sort of wore it everywhere we went, it was like sack cloth and ashes. It wasn't a very enjoyable year really."

The band began the 'Picture Tour' to promote the album, performing only songs from 'Faith' and a couple of numbers from 'Seventeen Seconds'. They soon began to discover that playing the same morbidly intense songs night after night was affecting them mentally, leaving them desolate and despondent. A sense of doom and fatalism hung over them. On some occasions, Robert even left the stage in tears.

The tour kicked off at Friars in Aylesbury and saw The Cure using a PA system which had been hired from Pink Floyd's sound equipment company, Britannia Row. It was ten times bigger than anything they had used before. It didn't detract, however, from the fact that the audiences wanted to hear 'Forest', '10.15 Saturday Night' and all the earlier songs with which they could now associate. They were to be disappointed. Instead of the normal diet of familiar numbers they were served up a liberal helping of gloom

and angst. A lot of the audiences reacted angrily, jeering and throwing cans at the stage.

On 22nd May, The Cure finished the tour by playing at the Dublin College May Ball where the gig was invaded by the local Dublin punks who broke through the security en masse to see them. They became very aggressive and the band endured twenty minutes of being 'canned' before they left the stage.

On 8th June, the band returned to Europe. Their first show was at the Stadthalle in Freiburg, West Germany, attended by less than 40 people! They then moved on to Holland, using a circus tent, in a bid to avoid playing the usual venues. The dates began well but, at Sittard on 24th June, Lol received a phone call just before they were due on stage, informing him that his mother had just died. They went on stage and played 'Faith', a perfect track for the tragic circumstances. The band returned to England the next day and played a tape of that concert at her funeral.

After a couple of weeks off, allowing Lol to be with his family, the tour restarted on 5th July in Werchter in Belgium. The show was a festival with Robert Palmer topping the bill. After The Cure had been on stage for only half an hour, a member of Palmer's crew threatened to turn down their sound if they didn't stop playing. Simon immediately shouted over the mike " Robert Palmer!, rock 'n' roll!" and the band proceeded to play a fifteen minute version of 'A Forest' stunning the audience and Palmer. Needless to say, when The Cure finally finished playing, Palmer's crew threw the band and their equipment unceremoniously off the stage.

On July, the band began recording their next single entitled 'Charlotte Sometimes'/'Splintered In Her Head' at Playground Studios - newly opened by Mike Hedges.

To accompany the single, the band, at the suggestion of Parry, retained the services of pop video maestro Mike Mansfield. Robert had an idea that the video should be a period setting and very mysterious and the band duly filmed it in an old, abandoned psychiatric hospital where there still remained a lot of padded cells. Unfortunately, the resulting video was an unmitigated disaster, totally inappropriate and rejected by the band. 'Charlotte Sometimes' has been hailed by some as one of The Cure's most effective singles although, when it was released some months later, it barely scraped into the Top 50, reaching No.44 in the charts.

The Cure headed back to America and embarked on their second US tour. The first two dates were at the New York Ritz after which, according to Simon, both he and Robert took an accidental overdose of quaaludes. A quaalude is a powerful hypnotic which, when taken in a prescribed dose, can produce feelings of euphoria before inducing sleep. Because it is such a powerful drug it can be extremely dangerous when mixed with alcohol often resulting in death. The pair were extremely lucky that they survived their binge with only unpleasant hallucinations and acute paranoia as side-effects.

However, the side-effects lasted for some days and the gigs they played on the West Coast seem to have been a complete blur. Robert later told Steve

Sutherland: "I think we then went straight to Pasadena and then to the Whiskey A Go Go in Los Angeles. I remember running to the hotel in tears after that gig so I must have been in a bad way. There were so many people backstage and they were all coming up to me and all I could see were faces...faces...faces. I think I was hallucinating.

"I kept imagining people were threatening me and I was still feeling weird when we arrived in Auckland, New Zealand! It was from the hotel in Auckland that I phoned up The Banshees. I called Severin - they were on tour in Scotland at the time - and I played him 'Charlotte Sometimes' down the phone. I was really proud of it. But, during the phone call, I fell asleep: the phone bill was $480. The next morning I was exhausted - and I couldn't understand how or why I was there." Ah, that's rock 'n' roll!

The band moved on to Australia and then crossed the Pacific once more where they played a string of dates in Canadian bars and cowboy clubs. Needless to say, they went down in Canada like the proverbial lead balloon.

After a couple of weeks' rest, The Cure set off again for France where their popularity had been growing fast. However, even the loyal French audiences weren't prepared for the moody depression of 'Faith' and, on 25th November, The Cure started another British tour, pleased to be home.

In America, 'Happily Ever After', a double album package of 'Seventeen Seconds' and 'Faith' was released on A&M Records. The LA Weekly wrote of the album: "Disciplined post punk from

one of the bands that helped forge the gloom movement."

The British tour opened at The Lyceum in Sheffield and ended on 3rd December at London's Hammersmith Palais. The band were supported by a diverse array of acts including: And Also The Trees and 1313 - an outfit consisting of Steve Severin and Lydia Lunch. Severin slept on Robert's hotel room floor to escape the misery of his grim bed and breakfast accommodation and the pair's already strong friendship strengthened further.

After a spell in a studio in Surrey called The Windmill where most of the demos for the next album were completed, Robert spent some time with Steve Severin in London, much to Simon's disgust. He had always been Robert's main confidant and felt threatened by Robert's close relationship with The Banshee.

In January 1982, Parry introduced Robert to various producers as they both felt that it was time for a change from Mike Hedges. Robert was convinced that the producer should be young and they finally settled on Phil Thornalley who fitted all the requirements.

The Cure were booked into RAK Studios between January and April and, for the first few days of the sessions, the atmosphere was tense. Robert was reasonably aggressive with

MEETINGS

THINGS I HAVE IN BASEMENTS (AND OFFICES SOMETIMES)

Thornalley who took no time at all criticising Robert's guitar sound. In addition, Thornalley would not tolerate Robert's tardiness, all of which made for a stormy relationship.

The pressure on Robert to produce their best album to this date was immense and he began to work twenty hours a day in the studio. Simon and Lol were able to use alcohol as a kind of release but, for Robert, however, it was not so easy. Sleeping on the floor of Fiction's offices to catch a few hours' sleep between sessions, he became manic, paranoid and obsessive. Occasionally he would loosen up and join in with the partying going on around him which, in turn, would render him incapable of doing anything for days on end. It was a vicious circle.

The album which finally emerged from those crazy, distorted days was entitled 'Pornography' and included the tracks: 'One Hundred Years', 'A Short Term Effect', 'The Hanging Garden', 'Siamese Twins', 'The Figurehead', 'A Strange Day', 'Cold' and 'Pornography'. The album cover again sported blurred images, although, on this occasion, the sleeve was colourful instead of a sombre grey. It was released to very mixed reviews. Sounds' Dave McCullough, previously a staunch Cure supporter, wrote: "I'd have to be very kind to like 'Porn' as liberal as a Cure fan. But the heavy handedness, the unfortunate turn of phrase, never mind the generally too obviously angst-sounding backing (a monotone of would-be despair), push The Cure to that periphery from whence they really ought to be trying to crawl.

MASTER

A FINISHED THING OR
SOMEONE WHO IS TOO DRUNK TO STAND

"'Porn' has too much music, too cluttered a backing for Smith's well-intended observance. There are too many 'nice hi-fi effects', there is a constant baulking away from the savage in the music, to project what Mr. Smith has to say.....While Cure fans are insidiously locked in The Cure (otherwise this musical crap wouldn't exist), Robert Smith seems locked in himself, a spiralling nightmare that leaves The Cure like (their once opponent) the Fall, a possible 'new progressive', making a pompous sounding music that is, when all's said and done, dryly meaningless."

ournalist Dave Hill observed: "The Cure have applied themselves to catching a related collection of the very purest feels endemic to their age, and holding them right on the spot in their intangible, unspecified, unmanageable and most unpleasant real form. Here is an album written from the knife edge of despair, and as a piece of craftsmanship in expressive sound, it is a very big, very harrowing achievement." Despite the opinion of the critics, 'Pornography' finally gave the band their first elusive Top Ten success, with the album peaking at No.8 in the UK charts.

The Cure went straight onto the 'Fourteen Explicit Moments' tour. Supported by Zerra 1, they played around the UK from 18th April to 1st May. The NME stated after witnessing their show at the Dome in Brighton on 21st April: "By the time they reach Hammersmith there'll be few groups this live or this powerful." A few dates later, Record Mirror noticed that

91

Robert's weight had escalated and quipped: "Robert Smith seems to be paying the price for his heaving boozing these days. He's getting quite chubby.. Better stick to your favourite Peruvian snuff, Rob - at least there's no calories in it."

The tour was dogged with problems and bad feelings from the start. It began with niggly little things which would be blown up out of all proportion such as Robert's objection to Parry's choice of tour manager. It soon became evident that cracks were beginning to appear in their fragile veneer. The band headed to Europe for a month and, after a show in Strasburg on 27th May, Robert and Simon had a violent argument resulting in them both walking out of the band. The altercation was finally settled but left pent up frustration, feelings of anger and hostility in its wake. Robert revealed later: "Things got worse the longer we played. At this stage we were really confronting people and the collective personality of the group completely changed. What had really been a jovial experience became an aggressive one, and there was real viciousness, real vindictiveness in some of the practical jokes that were being played.

"I didn't go out much. I tended to spend my time alone, at the hotel bar or in my room. I'd get drunk and end up sleeping in the bathroom and I wasn't myself, I hadn't really recovered. People couldn't speak to me because I wanted everyone to be as I was. You had to actually want to be part of it and people hated us, hated those concerts, even most Cure fans."

When the tour finished on 11th June in Brussels, Simon immediately quit the band, unable to cope with Robert's mood swings any longer and The Cure effectively dissolved. He was not to see Robert again for eighteen months.

In July, 'Hanging Garden'/'Killing An Arab' was released as a single and reached No.34 in the charts. It was released in 7" and 12" formats and also as a four-track double pack. The band, however, had gone their separate ways.

obert and his girlfriend Mary, whom he had dated since his teens, set off for a camping holiday in Wales, while Lol embarked on a vacation in Europe, both wanting time to themselves and, more importantly, time to recover. Neither could be contacted, which was just the way they wanted it.

Robert did, however, find some time for songwriting. The magazine Flexipop wanted The Cure to record a track which they could place on their cover and Robert wrote 'Larnent' for this purpose. The project proved therapeutic, taking place in the wilds of Wales with no outside pressures. On his return to London, he immediately went in to The Garden Studios and recorded the track in two days, accompanied by Mary and Steve Severin. For the first time in years he found the atmosphere in the studio relaxed and great fun.

Meanwhile, during Lol's holiday, he had made a decision to give up drumming and, on his return home, started taking piano lessons. He had decided that his drumming technique was limited and he had taken it as far as it would go.

IOB

RESIGNATION

He had, however, kept in close contact with Parry and the pair finally decided that something had to be done to bring The Cure back together. Subsequently, he called Robert and Lol together and asked them to write a fun single, something unlike The Cure which would break the mould and destroy the myth. The idea appealed to Robert and, with the former drummer with Wreckless Eric, Steve Goulding, they recorded 'Let's Go To Bed' and 'Just One Kiss'.

obert wrote the most lightweight lyrics that he could think of and gave the tracks what he saw as foolish titles. Musically, he tried to include everything that he despised. What Robert perceived as disposable, trashy pop, Parry immediately saw as potential hits and was determined to put 'Let's Go To Bed' out as a single. Robert was just as determined not to. Robert eventually conceded that if it was to be put out as a single, it should be released under a pseudonym. Parry disagreed and, where he would normally give in to Robert's demands, this time he stuck to his guns. His convictions on the subject were so strong, he even made a deal with Robert that if the single didn't make the Top Twenty, he would be released from his contract.

Having agreed that the record was to be released, it was a natural progression to shoot a video to accompany it. Parry had seen the showreel of a young video director called Tim Pope, whose videos for Soft Cell had met with some success. Parry was impressed and introduced him to Robert. Pope immediately liked Robert and, surprisingly, Robert felt the same way. Pope was recruited to produce the video and they began filming in a

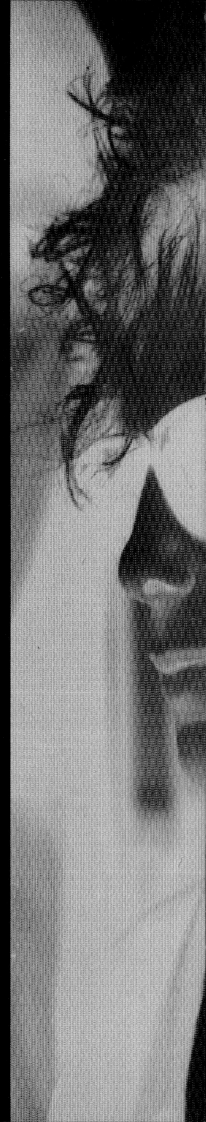

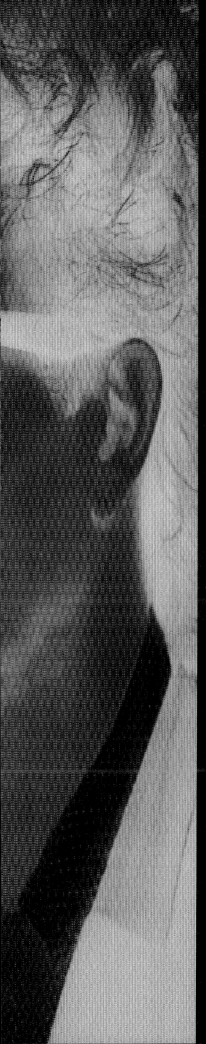

studio in St. John's Wood. In 'Ten Imaginary Years' Pope recalled: "I began to push him more and more because he had never performed in a video before. That's where we started to breed and develop that eccentric little character which we now all know and love! On the first take, he was very calm but on the second, I don't know why, I saw him as a clown - funny but also tragic."

This video produced for The Cure by Tim Pope was the first of many and the relationship which was forged between them then has endured until today. It has also been Pope's magnificently quirky videos which has been responsible, in part, for the band's meteoric rise to fame.

'Let's Go To Bed' was released in November and reached No.44 in the UK charts, Parry lost his bet and Robert immediately began the rounds of interviews, justifying and explaining the reasons behind its release. He told Melody Maker: "I just wanted to see if I could write a really dumb pop song that would get played on the radio because I hadn't written anything like that for ages and ages. It wasn't supposed to be a Cure single, it was supposed to be a solo single so that I just took the blame for it. I didn't want the name of The Cure to be tainted with a single like that, but there was a lot fo rows and bad feeling around that time and so it got released as The Cure. It wasn't commercial anyway. I realised it when I did it - which is why I lost interest in it - that it wasn't horrible enough, it just wasn't quite dumb enough to be commercial, it didn't even get played on the radio."

He explained to Record Mirror: "I don't think it's a Cure song. I wanted it released under a different name like we did with Cult Hero a couple of years ago. It's not that Cure songs are a formula but they do share a central core. This single has been released to get major daytime radio play and it's disappointing to me because it's the first time we've been seen to be involved in current trends or fashions. There are probably only a few thousand people who've held us up as an example to themselves but, if I were one of them, I'd feel let down. For us to be bothering in an arena I don't respect upsets me. When you spend time in a band trying to achieve certain goals, you don't want to betray them."

During the recording of 'Let's Go To Bed', The Banshees had come to the studio and invited him to play guitar on their British tour. He readily accepted, viewing it as a means of escape from The Cure and his responsibilities. Parry was furious.

To start with Robert agreed only to do the British leg of the tour but, when that concluded, he had become a full-time member. Parry was worried that the public would perceive Robert's stint with The Banshees as the end of The Cure and tried to extradite him through legal recourse. Robert sourly reminded him of the bet they had made before the release of 'Let's Go To Bed' and Parry backed down. Lol took a more philosophical approach. He knew that the day would come when Robert would, once again, want to sing and play his own songs. In the meantime, he was happy to wait.

During January and February 1983, The Banshees toured Australia, New Zealand and Japan with Robert handling the guitar parts. His place on the tour confused the press and fans alike and there was constant speculation on the future of The Cure.

In March they returned to London and Robert was approached by Royal Ballet choreographer, Nicholas Dixon, and invited to write the music for 'Les Enfants Terrible. Although Robert was intrigued, he was nervous of so great a task and suggested they tried out the idea on a Cure song. The song chosen was 'Siamese Twins' and the finished project was shown on BBC 2's Riverside with Lol on drums, Severin on bass, The Venomettes, of Soft Cell fame, on strings and accompanied by two dancers. Although it was met with considerable critical acclaim, neither Robert nor Dixon were pleased with it and the ballet project was indefinitely shelved.

Also in March, Robert and Severin finally worked on a project of their own. Called The Glove, it was intended to be a psychedelic pastiche and they went into Britannia Row studios to begin recording demos. They recruited Jeanette Landray, a dancer with Zoo and Budgie's girlfriend, to provide the vocals and then proceeded to spend the next four weeks in a disorientated, cultivated madness - staying in the studio until 5 or 6 in the morning which they followed by collapsing in Severin's flat watching bad horror movies. The resulting album which finally emerged from this collaboration was entitled 'Blue Sunshine', the name taken from such a film.

IMAGE

LIPS

Severin told Melody Maker: "The idea that The Glove could get away with anything vanished very quickly because it became a real responsibility to get it to sound not indulgent."

nexpectedly, in April, The Cure were invited to play live on BBC TV's Oxford Road Show. The appearance called for two tracks and Robert elected to play 'One Hundred Years' and 'Figurehead'. With Andy Anderson, drummer with Brilliant, and keyboard player Derek Thompson, Lol and Robert performed live for the first time since the departure of Simon. Robert realised just how much he missed it and decided then and there that The Cure should record once more.

Robert had an idea that the next recording would be very different from anything that had gone before. He wanted to experiment with sampling, sequencing and programming techniques and decided that the man to produce the single should be Steve Nye. Robert had heard Nye's work on Japan's 'Tin Drum' album and was mightily impressed. Robert said later of the experience: "I didn't care if it worked or not - no-one was expecting us to do anything anyway. It was a really funny way of working because we'd never done it before - sitting there, programming things, hearing them back straight away, putting down drum patterns and listening back to them without having to shout at a drummer! It was done quite fast - in under five days - and the actual recording itself was quite boring. But Jam Studios had a good pool table and a pretty garden with tables and chairs where I could write, and I learned a lot of technical things just from watching Steve Nye work."

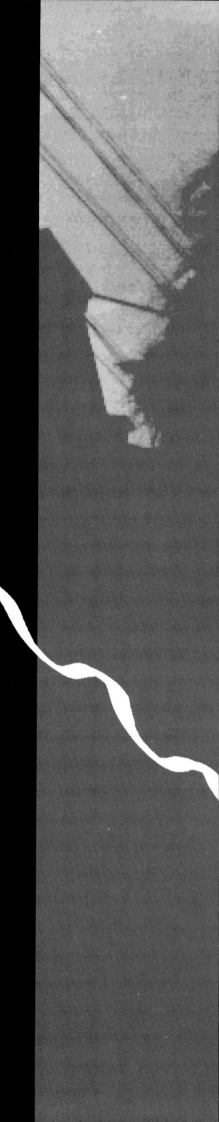

In July, the single 'The Walk'/'The Dream' was released, accompanied by a Tim Pope directed video. Pope explained: "We had this big toy box for Robert to take shirts out of and, as with all my videos, I tried to do it so that the images didn't correspond literally to the lyrics. I always try to make the film and the song work in parallel. In my head, I throw the song in the air and let in rest for a moment in my subconscious.

'Robert's lyrics are pretty esoteric - he follows his own logic and no-one can understand them as well as he does. The ideas of the old woman comes from there, she's around to interpret Robert's lyrics. My camera-man and assistants looked at me as if I was mad when we were shooting 'The Walk' so I knew the video was gonna be good. Oh, and the green stuff that droops around, sticky stuff...was all to do with rude things going on in the background...I think."

The single was an instant hit, peaking at No.12 and The Cure made two appearances on Top Of The Pops due to the BBC refusing the show the video. They were, apparently, worried that both Lol and Robert were wearing make-up and assumed they were gay. For the first appearance they appeared with drummer Andy Anderson and Porl Thompson on bass. Porl couldn't make the second show and Phil Thornalley stood in, happy to take some time out of the studio.

Melody Maker reviewed one of their appearances: "The Cure on Top Of The

Pops was an event almost as absurd as Jimmy Savile's insanity. They looked and acted bored, but all across the nation Cure fans, Cure converts and folk who can't tell The Cure from Culture Club and couldn't care less, interpreted Smith's stifled yawns as enigmatic arrogance. Such is the power of reputation, such is the impact of dressing in black."

At the same time, The Cure had been invited to headline Cornwall's outdoor festival, The Elephant Fayre. They accepted and with Phil and Andy, they played the gig as a four-piece, after warm up dates in Bournemouth and Bath.

The band were very well received at The Fayre but Robert felt that by playing live again, he had compromised The Cure's achievements and stated that, although he had wanted to play the old songs once more for nostalgic reasons, it would probably be the last time they would be performed. He claimed it was the end of an era.

aradoxically, Steve Sutherland, Melody Maker journalist and close friend of the band, wrote: "For one marvellous, all-too-brief midnight, The Cure were back and, thanks to the Fayre (easily Britain's best true "event"), we need no longer worry; they've assured us there's a Cure present and all the signs are that the Cure future will be well worth the wait." Curiouser and curiouser.

However, the answer to the annual 'Do the Cure exist?' question was answered positively when the band undertook a short American tour and then flew to France to record their next single, 'The Lovecats'. They used the Polydor-owned Studio Des Dames in

Paris and everyone agreed that the Parisian atmosphere and excellent ambience of the studio made the sessions the most enjoyable they had experienced. This enjoyment was reflected in the sparkley spirit of 'The Lovecats', a track totally removed from The Cure's usual style.

The single was mixed at Genetic studios by a young engineer, Dave 'Dirk' Allen, to whom Robert took an instant liking. Again, Tim Pope directed the video. According to Lol: "The funniest thing about making the video was the woman who looked after the cats. She looked more like a cat than any of her animals did. We had about thirty cats altogether and they wouldn't do anything we wanted them to. There was loads of cat food in strategic places to encourage them into the shot, but they hated the stuffed cats and they all ran away when we let them into the room."

Later in August, The Glove's single entitled 'Like An Animal' was released and, in September, Robert travelled to Italy with The Banshees to play in Rome after which they moved on to Venice where they filmed the Tim Pope-directed video for 'Dear Prudence'. A cover of The Beatles' track of the same name and taken from their 'White Album', the single was greeted with scepticism by the critics but, nevertheless, 'Dear Prudence' went straight into the UK

HOUR

AN ADULT MEASUREMENT OF TIME IN THE DAY

OTop Ten, peaking at No.3. The next stop on the tour was Israel, whilst, back in Britain The Glove's album 'Blue Sunshine was released.

On September 30th and 1st October, The Banshees headlined London's prestigious Royal Albert Hall. Both dates were televised and recorded for a forthcoming double album entitled: 'Nocturne'. The album was released in November to a complete bashing from the music press who saw the release of a double live album from the band described by the NME as "1978's most subversively stimulating band" as the repudiation of all that punk had stood for. Robert, for his part, felt the critics were unnecessarily harsh but stated that 'Nocturne' would have been better received had it been a single album.

On 25th October 'The Lovecats'/'Speak My Language' was released and the majority of the press loved it even if they found the new direction The Cure were apparently taking a tad confusing. The public also liked it and the single went into the charts at No.7. Some of the older, more die-hard Cure fans felt that the band had 'sold out' and Robert told Sounds journalist Bill Black:"Some (fans) feel really cheated, I really detest them. It's like we're their pet band and how dare I tamper with out mysterious image. I never asked for blind devotion. I resent it because they're trying to shrink me into a one-facetted person who's only allowed to produce one style of music. That's another reason why I wanted to do something totally stupid and off the wall."

He told ZigZag: "It's more exciting to be in The Cure now than it's ever been. There's less pressure because we can

now use it when we want to. There's less risk of becoming complacent than ever. The Cure don't have to make records ever again."

The success of the single meant the obligatory trip to Top Of The Pops. The band performed with the stage covered by dozens and dozens of cuddly toy cats and it was on this occasion that the crumpled grey suit which was to become their trademark made its first appearance. Robert forgot the words to 'The Lovecats' but even this usual Smith effort at subversion did not matter. They had a smash hit single, the army of Cure fans was growing daily and everyone was, for once, happy with life.

In the same month which saw The Cure riding so high in the charts, the second Glove single was released entitled 'Punish Me With Kisses' and was an unmitigated disaster, flopping unceremoniously. There was talk of a further Severin/Smith collaboration but, to date, it would seem it is not to be.

In December, an eight track mini album was released entitled 'Japanese Whispers' and it included the tracks: 'Let's Go To Bed', 'The Dream', 'Just One Kiss', 'The Upstairs Room', 'The Walk', 'Speak My Language', 'Lament' and 'The Lovecats'. It was, in essence, a compilation of the fantasy singles and their respective B-sides. The sleeve depicted cherubs and was Robert's own design.

During the special Christmas edition of Top Of The Pops, Robert appeared with both The Cure and The Banshees. Although the serious music press had known about and reported on The Cure for years, suddenly the band was big business. The media from the national newspapers to the glossy teen magazines were screaming for information about and running stories on the mysterious Cure, with particular emphasis being placed on Robert's private life.

Within a couple of months, the public knew - or thought they knew - more about Robert Smith than they had gleaned in the whole of the past six years. In interview after interview Robert deliberately set out to mislead the press, turning their own guns on them. If they wanted stories, he would give them stories and what stories they were! The press fell for them hook, line and sinker. To this day The Sunday Mirror still believes his parents take acid and his wife, Mary, is a stripping nurse.

he New Year brought two new albums for Robert to work on, his own and the forthcoming offering from The Banshees. Robert had stretched himself too thin and both sessions suffered. The Banshees' album, entitled 'Hyaena', had been started some ten months earlier and in that time The Cure had recorded 'The Lovecats' and 'The Walk', released 'Japanese Whispers', made a batch of videos and toured America. It was, according to the other Banshees, Robert's commitments with The Cure that was holding up their recording and, whilst Robert acknowledged that the situation was far from ideal, he felt he wasn't solely to blame accusing The Banshees of generally lacking direction and organisation.

Meanwhile, recording sessions for The Cure's album, 'The Top', were

being held at three studios, Trident, Genetic and Garden. Dave Allen took care of engineering the vocals, guitars and mixing whilst Howard Gray looked after drums, bass and additional guitars. Phil Thornalley's previous commitments as engineer for Duran Duran who were recording their 'Seven And The Ragged Tiger' album in Australia, made it necessary for Robert to play and compose all the basslines himself.

Robert revealed in 'Ten Imaginary Years': "As soon as 'The Top' was finished, I wanted bits of it to be different; but it was too late to re-record it because I was working to such absurd deadlines to keep The Banshees thing going as well. I'd never really had that before - an album always took as long as it took to make it good, but this time it had to be finished by a certain date and I was going back, stealing odd days out to overdub things thinking 'God, this ought to be faster' or 'that drum shouldn't sound like this'. It's not that I was unhappy with it, it's just that I could see the flaws."

'The Top' included the tracks: 'Shake Dog Shake', 'Bird Mad Girl', 'Wailing Wall', 'Give Me It', 'Dressing Up', 'The Caterpillar', 'Piggy In The Mirror', 'The Empty World', 'Bananafishbones', and 'The Top'.

Whilst Robert was battling with the hectic schedule of recording two albums, Porl Thompson had returned to the fold. He arrived at the studio one night to show the band his ideas for the sleeve artwork when Robert asked him if he would play sax on a track called 'Give Me It'. Subsequently, Porl was invited to provide sax, additional guitars and synths on the forthcoming Cure tour, a position which he readily accepted.

In March, The Banshees released their 'Swimming Horses' single and embarked on a short tour to promote it featuring an exhausted Robert on guitar. Relations were undoubtedly already strained but were compounded further by The Banshees' manager, Dave Woods, who felt that Robert should have left The Cure to become a full-time Banshee. The tour was not a happy one and became unbearable when Siouxsie sniped in an interview with Record Mirror: "Fat Boy Smith is nothing to do with the new album except he actually plays on it." Robert retorted: "I'm as much a member as I could be, but I don't have as much say as them. That's why it's always good when I go back to The Cure. I am The Cure."

On 30th March the single 'The Caterpillar'/'Happy The Man' was released along with a 12" format of 'Throw Your Foot'. One reviewer wrote: "Smith?...impossible. After the pastiche of 'Love Cats', a record so gorked on the cream of its own smugness it made motorists accelerate at any passing feline whenever it came on the car radio, the Cure scrape some new-found claws all over the vacant face of pop and out flows a truly distinctive alternative. A highly viable one as well.

"This song does everything wrong commercially and because of it sounds completely right. Acoustic guitars, violins, and a superpretentious lyric bursting with the kind of colour

GOD

FEAR OF DEATH

references which only spring from the
use of illegals, all on a voyage into the
human zoo. Brilliant."

Tim Pope's video which accompanied
the single portrayed the band playing i
a greenhouse with the both the band
and instruments coated in caterpillars.
Pope had originally wanted to use
butterflies but it was not the season fo
them and he has been recorded as
saying that the video was not one of h
best. However, the single shot straight
into the Top Twenty, settling at No.14.

On 3rd March, The Cure's next tour
had been announced, the tickets
selling out almost as soon as they wer
on sale. Due to this demand, the band
added a third night at London's
Hammersmith Odeon.

Also in March, Robert joined The
Banshees for a tour of Europe,
returning to Britain in time for The
Cure's second appearance on BBC
TV's Oxford Road Show. Phil
Thornalley was still in Australia with
Duran Duran so his place was
taken by Norman Fisher Jones.

During Robert's stint with The
Banshees, Lol kept himself busy b
producing And Also The Trees' 'Th
Secret Sea' and Baroque Bordello's
'Today'.

In April, The Cure's British tour
kicked off at the Edinburgh
Playhouse with Lol on keyboards,
Phil Thornalley back on bass, Porl
Thompson on sax, guitar and
additional keyboards and Andy
Anderson on drums. The tour
snaked around the country,
culminating with a show at Oxford's
Apollo and the three nights at the
Hammersmith Odeon. All four shows

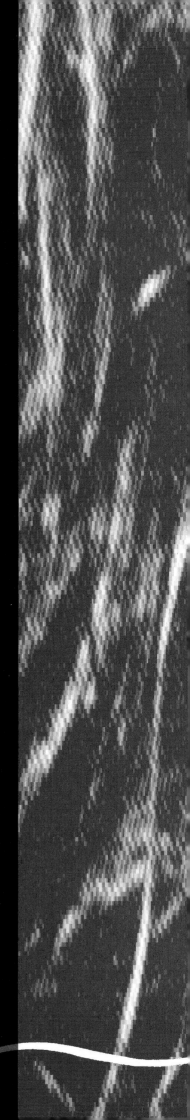

...were recorded by the Manor mobile for inclusion on a forthcoming live album entitled 'Concert'. Mick Brown reviewed one of the shows writing: "This is a performance built on fastidious perfectionism; the lighting is starkly effective; the use of film on a screen behind the stage hauntingly appropriate; the playing pristine and flawless. Seldom can an atmosphere of bleakness and futility have been conjured with quite such thorough professionalism." High praise indeed from a journalist who specialises in not being impressed!

Robert, meanwhile, continued his expert manipulation of the media telling the NME's Mat Snow his state of mind is "Happy but very muddled. I don't think it'll last - I just think I'm going through a mid-life crisis. The point where I stop working in contemporary music at all, I think, becomes increasingly close. In fact, it's very close. I just don't want to have bits of me falling off in public. I don't want to do it in front of the cameras."

He also claimed to the press that he had taken a live lamb on tour with him. Various reasons were given for this. In one interview he claimed he had found it in a hotel and, in another, he said it was given to him by a fan and was now living on his brother's Welsh farm. It is most unlikely that the lamb existed at all, but the press lapped the story up.

On 13th May, The Cure began a European tour following almost exactly in the footsteps of The Banshees two months earlier. Robert admitted that he found this confusing and was unable to concentrate on stage, often forgetting just which band he was with. He was exhausted, unable to sleep at night and suffering from severe panic attacks. He finally decided that he had no alternative but to quit The Banshees for the sake of his health. On 26 May, he telephoned Severin from Hamburg and informed him he could no longer fulfil his commitment to The Banshees. Although Severin was angry at the news, he detected the panic in Robert's voice and asked him to return to England to talk it through.

Robert cancelled two dates and flew back to London. However, instead of keeping his arranged meeting with The Banshees, he went directly to his doctor, who was horrified at his mental and physical condition. After recommending that Robert check into a health farm immediately, advice which he chose to ignore explaining he had to finish The Cure tour, his doctor wrote a certificate stating that Robert needed a complete rest. He sent the certificate to The Banshees and returned to Europe.

When the tour finally drew to a close he went to Wales with Mary for a much-needed break. Slowly he began to recover by taking long walks, playing football on the beach and spending time alone with Mary. After the vacation, he returned to The Cure with renewed vigour and enthusiasm, enhanced by the success of 'The Top' which had achieved the No.8 position in the UK album charts.

In August, Robert bought a basement flat in London's posh Maida Vale for himself and Mary. They moved in at once and then departed to Lake Windemere in The Lake District for another break. The quiet and seclusion of this chosen location was ideal for the task Robert had in mind. He listened to all The Cure's back catalogue and old songs in chronological order and chose

various tracks which he wanted to release.

Back in London, whilst he was mixing 'Concert', the live album recorded during the last British tour with Dave Allen, he saw an opportunity to release the tracks. He decided to put a selection of the old material together to appear as 'Curiosity - Cure Anomalies, 1977 - 1984', making the cassette version of 'Concert' a double package. 'Concert' included the tracks: 'Shake Dog Shake', 'Primary', 'Charlotte Sometimes', 'The Hanging Garden', 'Give It To Me', 'The Walk', 'One Hundred Years', 'A Forest', '10.15 Saturday Night' and 'Killing An Arab' with 'Curiosity' featuring: 'Heroin Face', 'Boys Don't Cry', 'Subway Song', 'At Night', 'In Your House', 'The Drowning Man', 'The Funeral Party', 'All Mine' and 'Forever'.

On 30th September, The Cure embarked on a World tour which opened in New Zealand. They were also scheduled to visit Australia, Japan, Canada and America. The first gigs went well and reasonably uneventfully but, when they reached Australia, they began to experience problems with Andy Anderson who was, allegedly, drinking far too much, causing him to become touchy and unreliable. After a heated altercation with Robert in Sydney he was let off with a caution but, after the second of their Japanese gigs, the drummer committed a crime of an altogether more serious nature.

After a night out in Tokyo with Robert, Andy had, quite literally, gone berserk, attacking fellow guests of the hotel as well as Parry, Phil and a number of security guards. He had eventually been overpowered and was placed under police guard. Robert fired him

immediately and The Cure departed for
San Francisco minus a drummer.

Phil Thornalley contacted an old friend
of his, former Psychedelic Fur drummer
Vince Ely, who was now resident in
San Francisco. Although he had not
drummed for over two years, preferring
to spend his time producing instead of
playing, he did a days' rehearsal and
then went on to do eleven shows with
The Cure, learning their numbers
during the soundcheck. Unfortunately,
although Vince proved to be an
excellent drummer, he had prior
production commitments and left the
tour in Texas. Once again Phil came to
the rescue, bringing in Boris Williams.

Boris, who had previously played with
Kim Wilde, had just finished a tour with
The Thompson Twins and was
spending some time in Los Angeles
with his girlfriend Cynde. After receiving
the call from Phil, he ran out, bought all
the Cure albums he could find and
proceeded to learn the songs. He
explained in 'Ten Imaginary Years':
"Actually, it wasn't too hard to learn
their songs once I knew how they
started and how they finished! Ha ha! It
was a big change for me - really
refreshing. At last I was really playing
the drums. With the Twins it was all
electronic and precise whereas The
Cure gave me more freedom and they
were creative and fun."

Boris was immediately accepted by the
band who liked him enormously and
respected his playing. After the last

GLANCE

THE BEST LOOK OF ALL — OFTEN
THROUGH CLOSING DOORS OR DRAWING CURTAINS

show, in New York, Robert invited Boris to look on The Cure as a long-term project, urging him not to go back out on tour with The Thompson Twins. After initial doubts due to the drop in salary he had experienced whilst working with The Cure, Boris accepted.

During the American tour, Robert was reported to have told Shake magazine: "I lie a lot. To lie to gain someone's confidence or to get close to someone is a bit stupid. I made things up but just through boredom a lot of the time. I mean, a lot of what goes on in The Cure is just completely made up anyway. We spend a lot of time just talking rubbish at each other." No doubt Shake magazine believed him!

He later told Record Mirror: "I lie a lot, people know I do and sometimes they stand there horrified at me. If we go away or if we're being taken out by people, I just create whole mythical worlds about me, never repeating the same anecdote twice.

"I really hate being in the company of people who take themselves seriously. I always have done but it's become pathological now. I can't stand people who sit and talk to me in a very serious way. When I go abroad, I'll do three interviews in one country and give three different answers to all three, knowing that many people will read all of them and they won't be able to take you seriously because the whole thing is so absurd."

Also during this tour, Robert stopped smoking saying : "I just decided that I should. I hate dependency on physical things and didn't want to get to the stage where I had to have a cigarette. I can't remember ever wanting to give up

drink, though. I think I've been drunk every night this year."

In October, whilst the band were still in America, 'Concert' was released. Because it had been recorded on a low budget it lacked the polish that some live albums have. It contained very few overdubs and, consequently, sounded totally honest. Melody Maker's Steve Sutherland wrote: "Not solely a souvenir, not a makeweight, not an indulgence, the 'Concert' package is a fresh perspective on a band captured at its creative peak and, as such, deserves a place alongside any album, Cure live or otherwise, that you care to cherish."

'Concert' went straight into the UK album charts and reached No.26.

Christmas 1984 came and went without much ado. Robert told one magazine: 'Nowadays Christmas Day itself always seems to end up as an anti-climax. You spend it at home, wallowing in food and drink and then you feel ill for days afterwards.

'I don't give parties, although I do gatecrash other people's sometimes. But the idea of parties is usually a hundred times better than the realisation. You end up looking around at the people there and wishing 90% of them were dead and you think 'What the fuck am I doing here?' And then there's all those Christmas singles…I like Christmas singles - but only if I've had about fifteen pints and I'm slumped over a table. I can't imagine us ever making one."

Early in the New Year, the band took some time off from the constant grind of touring. Robert began to think about making the

next album and also contemplated the current line-up of the band.

hil Thornalley had never considered himself a permanent member of The Cure. He had taken over the bass slot to help the band out but saw himself primarily as a recording engineer and producer. During his time on the road he had gained invaluable experience but felt that it was time to return to studio work. Despite several invitations from Robert to stay with The Cure for, at least, the following year, Thornalley decided to quit. Although the departure was amicable at the time, it has been documented that Thornalley later regretted this decision.

A few months previously, Robert had once again met up with Simon Gallup who had formed a band called Fools Dance without much success. They both decided to bury the hatchet regarding their previous differences and Robert invited Simon to rejoin The Cure.

In March the band went into Angel Studios with Dave Allen to commence recording their new album. Although Simon was nervous of playing with Boris and Porl, the sessions went well. Robert explained: "We played pool a lot and had fun. The atmosphere was stupid, almost childish and we were in a hurry to get back in the studio every day. With Simon, the excitement came back and the band was more aggressive, more vital. He knew me so well that I didn't really need to explain anything to him. We drank a lot more than at any other recording session but this time we didn't take any drugs."

This album took a particularly long time to record and, after a month, the band transferred to The Townhouse studio complex in London's Shepherd Bush. The album which finally emerged was entitled 'The Head On The Door' and included the tracks: 'In Between Days', 'Kyoto Song', 'The Blood', 'Six Different Ways', 'Push', 'The Baby Screams', 'Close To Me', 'A Night Like This', 'Screw' and 'Sinking'.

In March Robert gave an in-depth interview to ZigZag's Antonella Black, explaining his views on, amongst other things, drugs. "They're good fun, but, they give you a different perspective on things. I know people who have taken lots of drugs, and I don't consider their consciousness as having expanded at all; but then again, they may think it has, so it may well have done. Drugs haven't changed my outlook on anything; but no one particular thing has. My favourite drug is alcohol."

n his relationship with his girlfriend he said: "My relationship with Mary is what most people would consider to be 'liberal' - but not in that horrible contrived sense. We spend a lot of time apart. If I'm on tour, she doesn't come with me because she doesn't like that side of it. She remembers when nobody wanted to talk to me. She can see the hypocrisy of the whole situation - as I can -but obviously it's far more difficult for someone who is close to me to cope with it. People tend to ignore her and think she's just another fan. She doesn't tolerate that, and nor do I. We understand each other, which is why we've been together for so long. There's very little which needs to be said, which I like. Sometimes it's glamorous and romantic - which is fun - but only if you don't take it seriously. Love should never be taken seriously."

FEAR

WANTING TO BE STRONG

Robert made quite an impression on Black who also noted: "Robert is anything but the vague, listless bambast merchant he has been portrayed as. He is witty, articulate, delicious, and very funny. A gentleman far more aware of his environs than a number of people presume. He is NOT a fat man with a silly haircut and a languid guitar. Admittedly, he has the chronic habit of fixating on his feet, but he is, in a nutshell, utterly delightful."

In June, the new line-up played live for the first time in Barcelona and the show was filmed. Their first concert in Spain, they were fuelled with plenty of Sangria, played a storming gig and the audience went wild. From Spain they travelled to Italy, playing a gig supported by The Associates. On 27th July, they played third on the bill at a festival in the Antic Panathinaikos in Athens. Other bands featured included Nina Hagen, Talk Talk and Telephone. The Cure stole the show with their near legendary performance and won the hearts of dozens of thousands of Greek fans. The whole show was filmed and broadcast throughout Europe later on in the year.

Back in Britain, a single entitled 'In Between Days'/'The Exploding Boy' had been released, taken from the forthcoming album. It was met with rave reviews everywhere, cropping up in more than one magazine as 'Single Of The Week' and being hailed as their best tune since 'The Lovecats'. Sounds' hack, Carole Linfield, felt: "You will never have a straightforward Cure song. While Robert insists that 'In Between Days' is totally coherent, it's surely as close as they'll get to, well, a love song."

In any event, the public liked this "completely and irresistably loveable tune" and the single shot into the charts at No.15. The video, naturally, was directed by Tim Pope and depicted wild, fluorescent socks dancing around between the band. Robert told Sounds: "It all began when I said to the video director, Tim Pope, that we'd like flashes of colour going between my head when I was singing, and he said, 'What, colour like this, like my socks' and I said 'yeah'. That obviously stuck in his mind because socks are cheap and easy to come by.

"He tells us that he told the animators to use fluorescent socks as the colour scheme and they took him at his word. And they spent thousands of pounds drawing all those socks frame by frame - bloody mental! £8,000! It's outrageous. Then it was all done and I got this anguished phone call apologising. At first I hated it, then I came round to it, but now I'm fed up with it because its obliterated the idea of the video."

In late August the album 'The Head On The Door' was released to critical acclaim and peaked in the album charts at No.7. Steve Sutherland wrote in Melody Maker: "Certainly, 'The Head' is as certifiable as 'The Top' in the (non) sense that it's as wilfully enigmatic as ever. The only difference is it's determinedly languorous, nowhere near as tortured or tense as its predecessor and for all its deliberate variety and characteristic quirks, it maintains a disturbingly even strain."

Suddenly, Robert Smith's face adorned the covers of dozens of different magazines and newspapers. He is a star! He is a god! He is a sex-symbol! He is a genius! the headlines

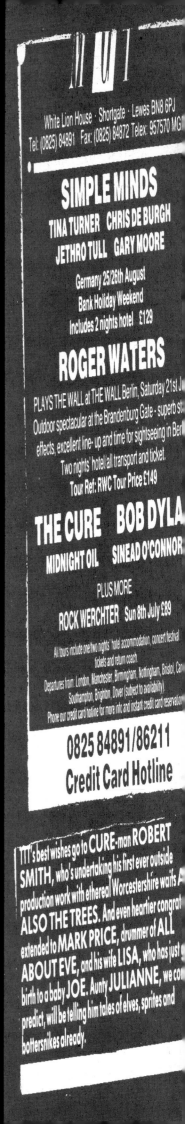

screamed. Everybody wanted a different angle on the same story and Robert, only too happy to please, gave them one. Explaining the title of the album he told Sounds that it represented a Punch & Judy show where a puppet's head rolls off. He told Smash Hits it came from a recurring nightmare he had as a child of a horrible grinning man who'd appear on top of the bedroom door and laugh. And so it went on.

Robert told Record Mirror: "I prefer this record to 'The Top', it's a bit easier for me to like so I imagine it's easier for everybody else to like as well. Because I played all the instruments on 'The Top' - except the drums, it was easy to get carried away in a dense mixture of sounds but on this one, all five of us were there so there was a lot more communication of ideas. Eight of the songs are first takes which is something we haven't done since we made 'Seventeen Seconds' which as everybody knows was the fastest record ever made."

Robert gave an astonishingly frank interview to cynical Fiona Russell-Powell of The Face magazine. On drugs he told her "The last time I did acid was at Christmas. The first time I tried it was with Severin a few years ago and I was fucking devastated for a week! I think they were God pills! It was clear light-blue gelatine tablets from America. Jobson was there as well. I think he's the funniest person I've ever met. Anyway, it was snowing and all the world was white. I suffered quite a lot.

"But, no, I don't take a lot of drugs, although 'The Top' was pretty drug-orientated, but only 'cos it was fun. The thing is, I never change at all after

taking LSD, no matter how many times
I take it. It hasn't changed or altered my
perception of the world at all, which is
what it does to some people. In that
sense, I've always had a very distorted
view of reality, my sense of values has
always been the same. When I tripped
for the first time I realised that it was
just like I was anyway. I stopped taking
it in the end because I felt sick and got
a headache. It's like drinking. You get
drunk for different reasons. You can
get socially drunk or you can get drunk
on your own and get very morbid and
tedious....Drinking's recreational, I
think. I used to get drunk on my own a
lot but I don't anymore."

On his smudged, red-lipsticked lips that
had become his trademark, Robert
explained: "Ah, the lipstick. I don't put it
on properly because people would
think I was doing it for reasons of vanity
whereas I do it for reasons of
theatricality. I used to wear it when we
did 'Pornography', I used to wear red
lipstick all round my eyes and all round
my mouth, so that when we were on
stage, I'd sweat and it'd all run so it
would look like someone had punched
me in the mouth and my eyes were
bleeding. I had to stop it though
because my eyesight started to suffer. I
kept the lipstick because it's so out of
character for me to do something like
that." Out of which character, he failed
to explain.

Robert also explained how he achieved
his increasingly dishevelled
appearance to Just 17 readers: "I don't
worry too much about it. I mean, I
haven't washed my hair for three and a
half weeks. I always use gel, not
hairspray. It's called KMS or something
and it comes with hexagrams on. It's
got the most glue-like consistency of
anything I've ever come across. I back

combe it a lot too. I did use mousse for a while but it used to drip onto my nose in big globs when I was on stage, which was disgusting."

The Cure were, by this time, massively successful throughout the world (Smith's popularity in France was only rivalled by Bowie and, perhaps, Jagger) with only America remaining unimpressed by Smith and Co's talent. This, however, was to change with the release of 'The Head On The Door' a few weeks after that of its European counterpart. The album went straight into the US charts, peaking at No.59. Cracking the biggest and most lucrative of all territories was now well within The Cure's grasp.

In September, 'Close To Me'/'A Man Inside My Mouth' was the second single from the album to be released, making No.24 in the UK charts and complimented by an acclaimed claustrophobic Pope directed video.

To promote both the single and the album, The Cure embarked on another British tour, culminating in a show at Wembley Arena. Jack Barron, writing for Sounds, reviewed the gig: "A soothing interval to have a mulled whine over whether The Cure have become part of The Disease. I don't think so. Robert Smith is beyond the pale of the

FAILING

AN INEVITABLE

likes of Nik Kershaw or King. He makes Top Of The Pops watchable: turns it into a lipstick scarred, stubbly, greasy, shabby song of fear. Then... God flips a switch and blows out the electric candles. 'The Baby Screams' and so do the audience. I'm slightly amazed that The Cure can fill this Arena, but not for long. Before the man with the untucked shirt and volcanic hair can sing 'Strike Me Dead', the hall is alive with a rush stagewards, with unbridled enthusiasm. This is a sign of the times."

The British tour completed, The Cure crossed the Atlantic for a short but successful tour of America. The highlight of this outing was a sold-out show at Radio City in New York. David Fricke reported: "Compared to the pouting humourless Cure that had previously played New York, the Smith Gang on this trip often let its icy cool drop in strange, unexpected ways. During 'Let's Go To Bed', Smith bounced around in front of the mike in a comic ragamuffin dance. The driving pulse and epic chime of the guitars in 'Push' never stampeded over the song's sweet pop outreach and, in the final encore, The Cure went totally teenage with an unexpected brontosaurus stomp through Gary Glitter's 'Do You Wanna Touch Me'. Smith gone glam? What fun!"

On their return, The Cure played Camden Palace in aid of MENCAP, the charity for the mentally handicapped. The concert was filmed and part of the show was broadcast live by BBC TV's Old Grey Whistle Test.

The Cure found the MENCAP show particularly difficult due to the fact that they had become used to playing large venues and outdoor festivals. In a venue as small as the Camden Palace the band are very close to the audience and this made Robert extremely nervous.

In December, the band played a number of dates in France and then returned to Britain for a well-earned Christmas break.

n early 1986, The Cure's contract with Polydor was up and due to be renegotiated. Robert thought it probable that the record company would want to put out a singles compilation album to monopolise on their recent success. To ensure that he had full control over any such release, Robert decided to plan a compilation himself. The band re-recorded 'Boys Don't Cry' and, in association with Tim Pope, put together an accompanying collection of Cure videos.

Pope was documented as saying in Ten Imaginary Years: "While we were putting it together, whever Smith went out of the room, I'd always manage to have 'Charlotte Sometimes' on the screen when he came back in. And what I admire about him is he didn't care - he decided to put the whole thing out, just taking the piss. That's what I like about Smithy, he's a very paradoxical character. Everything he is, he isn't. He's very pretentious but he isn't. He's always black yet he's white and The Cure are one of the stupidest bands you could ever work with yet they're the brightest, the most intelligent. They're the noisiest but they can be the quietest - that's what I love about them. Robert says he's like a

child but he isn't, he's too intelligent."

In April, 'Close To Me' was riding high in the French charts requiring The Cure to appear on a French TV show. 'Champs Elysee' is a France's answer to both Wogan and Top Of The Pops and is seen live by 15 million viewers. Boris and Porl were on vacation. Consequently, Robert, Simon and Lol travelled to Paris with Martin, Lol's flatmate, who had been recruited to mime keyboards and Record Mirror journalist Elenor Levy.

On their spectacular success in France Lol commented to Levy: "The same way we started in England, we started here. I think there's a bit more respect for us because of it. We're almost adopted sons; we're not an English group coming to play in France. We're a group they've known over the years. I think people have this horrible English attitude when they go abroad and say 'well, you must like us, we're British'. We've never had that attitude because we went to different countries at the very beginning before we were known in Britain."

On 25th April, The Cure played The Royal Albert Hall, headlining Sound

COLOUR

SEA-BLUE (AS THE SUN COMES UP)
SKY- GREY (BEFORE BIG RAINDROPS)
NIGHT- BLACK (THINKING)

Waves,the week-long benefit for Greenpeace. Elenor Levy was there: "The Cure managed something only the last night of the proms is rumoured to do. They got the Albert Hall moving. Queen Victoria must be turning in her grave."

The Cure's new, updated version of 'Boys Don't Cry' was also released in April backed by two unlikely tracks - 'Do The Hansa' and 'Pillbox Tales'. In America, 'Let's Go To Bed' was released as the A-side, with 'Boys Don't Cry' demoted to the B-side. This time around, the wonderful 'Boys Don't Cry' reached a healthy No.22 in the UK charts resulting in another appearance on Top Of The Pops. The accompanying video, directed naturally by Pope, featured the original trio of Smith, Tolhurst and Dempsey playing behind a screen while three small boys mimed their parts.

May saw the release of 'Standing On A Beach' a compilation of singles spanning seven years and included the tracks: 'Killing An Arab', '10.15 Saturday Night', 'Boys Don't Cry', 'Jumping Someone Else's Train', 'A Forest', 'Play For Today', 'Primary', 'Other Voices', 'Charlotte Sometimes', 'The Hanging Garden', 'Let's Go To Bed', 'The Walk', 'The Love Cats', 'The Caterpillar', 'In Between Days', 'Close To Me' and 'A Night Like This'.

'Staring At The Sea', Pope's video compilation was released simultaneously. For the diehard Cure disciples these pearly compilations were a must but, even for the more sceptical they were, at the very least, an interesting set which documented Robert's prolific career with exceptional clarity. Smash Hits best described the experience of viewing the video

collection: "In the space of one hour, Robert Smith changes from a fresh-faced, clean cut youth into the shambling, unkempt figure of today which is a bit of a weird trip (man)."

Video World wrote: "What makes it different from your average run of the mill video? Well, I'll tell you. Haircuts. In the end it's the sheer joy of watching sprouting locks on the move, particularly in the case of singer Robert Smith. First off it all looks quite normal, if a little ruffled, but by the time they get round to 'Love Cats' and 'The Caterpillar', we are talking major hair-dos. And very exciting it is too."

With the release of the compilations, the media onslaught began again and Robert's haystack hairstyle and face, complete with eyeliner, lipstick and five o'clock shadow, glared from the front covers of dozens of magazines and the stories began to circulate. He told Sounds' hack Glyn Brown: "Remember Pope Paul, the little wizened one with the bald head? I met him. My father had an audience with him."

The retrospective 'Standing On A Beach' album achieved The Cure's highest chart position to that date at No.4. The album was released in America some weeks later and made No.48 in the US album charts.

At the end of May, Robert went alone to America to promote the album and a tour, scheduled for July. The reason behind him making this sojourn alone gave rise to the theory that Robert Smith was now The Cure or, at least, the only band member that anybody wished to talk to. Certainly, he told Aquarian Weekly: "I could have brought the whole band but it would have cost a lot more and they would have just gone out and got pissed and I would still have had to do the interviews on my own."

fter a promotional tour of European TV shows and an appearance at the Pink Pop Festival in Holland, The Cure staged another effective publicity stunt. In order to appear at a show in Verona, the band and their girlfriends booked a carriage on the luxurious Orient Express, bound for Venice, at a cost of £15,000. They were also accompanied on the trip by most of Fleet Street and a film crew from BBC TV's Old Grey Whistle Test. After they had set off, Italian fire officials fortuitously cancelled the gig, providing the band with the perfect excuse for a holiday - the drunken highlights of which were screened on June 17.

David Wigg of The Daily Express, an unlikely Cure fan but a man whose love for champagne lunches in lavish surroundings is legendary was told by Robert: "We did not always travel around in this kind of style. When we first started we travelled around in an old Bedford van we bought for £45, held together by tape and chewing gum. I have always wanted to travel on this train and now we have the opportunity to do so."

On their return, the band began rehearsing and recording some twenty new numbers for their next album, tentatively titled 'One Million Virgins' and then went to Germany for the inevitable round of summer festivals.

On 21st June, they made their second

major appearance in the UK , headlining the Glastonbury CND Festival. One reviewer reported: "The Cure's set is their well-trodden fait accompli of recent months. Standing on a beach and sobbing out 'the hits', even if it means 6,427 encores. So many cats and cupboards and fingerclicks. Close indeed, and cute and coy, and if popular bands must only perform shows that have the intimacy of a cashpoint machine, then at least let them do it with gallons of white light in blackness. As here, Smith and his backing band (let's face it) nobly attempt. 'One Hundred Years' is the only song in the world that lasts as long as its title without ever falling below the 'admirably magical' level."

In July, The Cure travelled Stateside for the beginning of their American tour, opening at the Great Woods Centre For The Performing Arts in Mansfield. The Boston Globe wrote: "With the possible exception of Pink Floyd, no rock band has ever put across such compelling sadness."

Executives at the band's American record company, Elektra, were pleased by the success of both 'The Head On The Door' and 'Standing On A Beach' and decided to re-release 'Let's Go To Bed' despite strong opposition from Robert. He had wanted 'Boys Don't Cry' to be released as the single but finally compromised by releasing it on the B-side. He told Only Music: "I've given up fighting with the record company in America. As long as they release the album and don't mess about, I don't really care what they release as the single because we never sell a lot of singles anyway, so what difference does it make."

The American media became as

fascinated with Robert as the British were. He gave dozens of interviews to a diverse array of publications including Creem, Rolling Stone, Musician, BAM and LA Weekly. They were captivated by what they saw as "The male Kate Bush, the thinking teen's pin-up, the security blanket of the bedsit set, a dark version of Boy George and the next Thompson Twins." Robert had further attracted the media's attention by hacking his infamous volcanic hairstyle down to a crew cut. Only Music asked: "Can it be that the entire world as we know it is in an uproar over Robert Smith's hair? A haircut is hardly a major news event...or is it? MTV, at least, broadcast special bulletins nearly every hour when the former mop-top chopped his locks off."

Robert said to Melody Maker, by way of explanation: "I was fed up with people saying 'God, how did you get your hair like that?' So I thought 'I'll get you' and had it cut off. The paradox, of course is that now people talk about the hair even more. It's all they talk about. Everyone hates it. I hate it most. It's the most unattractive haircut. I just about recognise myself in the mirror now it's grown a little. Still, it makes no difference to me and, if it does to other people, well I hope they die."

However, Dave Kendall hit on a more likely explanation when reviewing their

CITY

DIRTY, NOISY, CROWDED, STIFLING, AIRLESS, BUSY, DRAB, IMPERSONAL

gig at The Pier in New York: "And the only thing missing is Robert Smith's hair. Maybe we can put it down to a good business decision - rednecks don't like freaks. Middle America here they come. No more hairy Bob."

Whilst the whole of America was busy debating the trivial subject of Robert's hair, their visit to Los Angeles was tainted by a particularly unpleasant incident. Seconds before the band were due to appear on stage, a fan named Jonathan Morland made a bizarre suicide bid in the audience, whilst other fans cheered him on thinking his death attempt was part of the act. After stabbing himself repeatedly in the chest and stomach with a seven-inch hunting knife, Morland was taken to hospital where his condition was reported as "critical". Police later found a suicide note in his car in which he stated he wanted to kill himself because of his hopeless love for a girl called Andrea. A spokesman for The Cure stated at the time: "It was a bitter ending for them because it happened on the last night of what had been a successful US tour. They could not believe that anyone would do that at one of their gigs."

After America, The Cure played one show in Spain and four in France. The last two shows, on 9th and 10th August were held in a Roman Amphitheatre in Orange, Provence. The Cure's shows were the first at the venue since Dire Straits played there two years previously and provided a wonderful backdrop for Tim Pope, enabling him to film live footage for what was his first attempt at a full length feature on The Cure.

When the shows and the filming was over, The Cure took time out in Toulon.

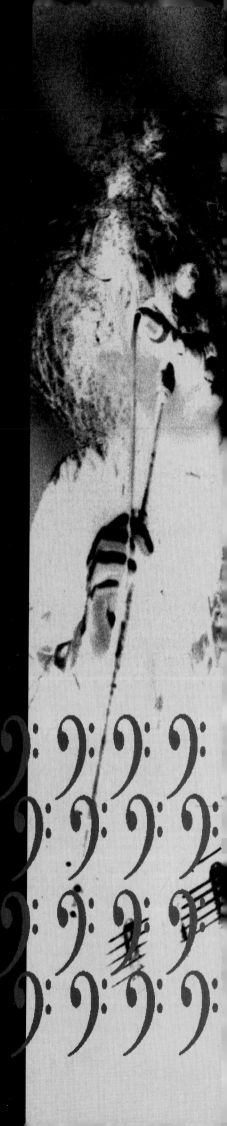

The object of the exercise was to sample some peace and quiet but the holiday turned into a disaster. The local paper had disclosed the band's location and their hotel was under siege by fans, rendering it impossible for them to leave their hotel rooms.

After escaping from Toulon, the band withdrew to Jean Costa's studio in Draguignan to begin work on the songs they had demo'd earlier in the year. The reason for remaining in France, it seems, was to avoid the tax man. Robert revealed: "If I've got the choice, I'd rather pay no tax. I'm not very materially minded - the first thing I bought when I had any money out of The Cure was the biggest bed I could find, then I bought a jeep, then after that there was absolutely nothing else that I wanted. But we play concerts for CND and Greenpeace, and I find it very disagreeable that 60% of what I pay in tax is spent on military and defence. I'd rather have the money so that I can use it selfishly or use it for other people or for other things if I want to."

The demoing completed, the band then drove to a studio-cum-vineyard at Miraval in the South of France. Again, the French atmosphere appeared to have a positive effect on the band. Robert told Melody Maker's Steve Sutherland: "We recorded at least a song a day, sometimes two. Most of them were first takes, almost jamming the songs to get the feel right. We spent a couple of hours playing each song so we became familiar with it and then recorded it in one go and it worked! It was a delight to record, a joy."

Sutherland then asked Robert if the fact that the studio had its own vineyards helped. Robert replied: "Oh,

that and the fact that I had loads of
words. Usually I get really stuck but I
had words for twenty-three songs and I
think they're easily the best I've ever
written. I astounded myself. I wrote the
songs the way I wrote 'The Walk'. I had
a mood for each song and I sifted back
through what I'd already done and a
couple of songs even refer to incidents
I've already written songs about but
they actually capture the spirit of them
far more."

The Cure spent three creative months
at Miraval and the resulting double
album was entitled 'Kiss Me Kiss Me
Kiss Me' and included the tracks: 'The
Kiss', 'Catch', 'Torture', 'If Only Tonight
We Could Sleep', 'Why Can't I Be You',
'How Beautiful You Are', 'Hey You!',
'Snakepit', 'Just Like Heaven', 'All I
want', 'Hot Hot Hot!!!', 'One More
Time', 'Like Cockatoos', 'Icing Sugar',
'The Perfect Girl', 'A Thousand Hours',
'Shiver And Shake' and 'Fight'.

Although, at the time, the location

CHILDHOOD

THE HAPPIEST OF TIMES -
EVERYTHING BIGGER & BRIGHTER & LIG

CLOSER

seemed idyllic and everything in the garden appeared rosy, it later emerged that cracks were beginning to appear in Robert's hitherto perfect partnership with Lol. He was allegedly drinking to the point of alcoholism and Robert issued an ultimatum. Lol made the first of several visits to a health farm to 'dry out'.

Robert revealed some years later: "I was friends with him, but I was never really really close. I was best friends with Simon. Lol was just there. He was there as a safety valve really, to get rid of unwanted tension. From 1985 onwards I never had a conversation with Lol because we disagreed about virtually everything. His friends were city beerboys driving about in silver Porsches. The whole social side of his life was anathema to what me and Simon liked. We disagreed about everything. He voted Conservative, he voted for law and order...all the things we used to joke about." Robert also accused Lol of alcoholism. "Everyone was disgusted by his behaviour. He became a victim and it was a downward spiral."

However, in 1986, the band carefully papered over the cracks and displayed a consolidated front the world. No one outside the band was any the wiser.

From France, Robert flew with Dave Allen to Compass Point Studios in The Bahamas to mix the album. Allen revealed: "As it turned out we had such a limited time that we were doing two mixes a day, and so we booked more time at ICP Studios in Brussels to finish off a few weeks later."

The mixing complete, Robert then flew to Eire where he was joined by the rest of the band and they prepared for their forthcoming South American tour with intensive rehearsals. Tim Pope also flew over to shoot a video for the 'Why Can't I Be You' single. The video portrayed the band, in fancy dress, participating in clumsy choreographed sequences with Robert dressed as some sort of furry animal. He later revealed in Select that he was wearing a headless bear costume: "A fan said to me, 'I wish I could be you'. In the song I turned that around. I wanted to be a polar bear but I refused to wear the head. We filmed the dancing in Dublin. We met this Irish dancing teacher in a bar the night before who looked like Alistair Sim but more manic: she showed us some steps. The obvious phonetic depiction of the word "can't" (a pair of lips) was nothing to do with me - it's the childish side of Tim Pope's award-winning nature."

Pope smirked: "This is it! This is the video I've always wanted to make. The Cure dancing! I can't believe I'm seeing this! They're finished!"

The South American tour kicked off in March with a show at the twenty thousand capacity Buenos Aires Football Stadium, the scene of severe rioting when the gig proved to be over-subscribed. Over one hundred people where arrested and the security for the tour was immediately taken over by the Ministry Of Interior Affairs. Once again, they found themselves confined to barracks. Robert explained: "It's like what happened to us in France -

Robert Smith

Full name - Robert Smith
Date of birth - 21 April 1959
height - 5 ft 10 ins
Weight - 11 stone
Colour of eyes - blue (sometimes grey)
Town of origin - Blackpool
Educated - Sometimes
qualifications — some 'O' levels. some 'A' levels
hobbies - all below & more
Likes - Sleeping preferably 16 hours at a time
....and reading
dislikes - waking, mad bob, dehydration
Previous Jobs - Christmas Postman .1977
Favourite Food - Vegitarian and Indian
Favourite drink - lager and orange, Cold milk and vanilla
Favourite Music - Classical and Indian   Earl grey Tea
Favourite bands - Joy division, Cocteau Twins, Echo and the Bunnymen
the Magic band
Favourite films - 2001, one Flew over the cuckoos nest, Eraserhead
Apocalypse now, Taxi driver, Mad max II, Gentlemen prefer
blondes, Whatever happened to Baby Jane?, Re-animator.
Favourite T.V. - night thoughts, news, Minder, Sky at Night,
Late night film, Man from Uncle
Favourite actress - steadman, monroe, Divine!, A. hepburn, Bow, leigh, Davis,
Crawford, Kinski, Poole
Favourite actor - De niro, nicholson, Gibson, Curtis, lemmon, Matthau, Eastwood
Ford, H Fonda, Mcdowell.
Favourite Books - les Enfant terrible, Cocteau, Gormenghast trilogy,
Peake - Lolita' nabokov, Something Wicked this way Comes - Ray Bradbury
Favourite author - Camus, Kafka, Peake, Cocteau, Salinger, Thomas,
Football team - Brazil, Player - Glen Hoddle.
Best live Show Seen - Tommy Cooper. S.A.H.B

we've suddenly become the biggest international group. We were met at the airport by limos and television crews and stuff! The hotel was besieged by millions of people, we were signing autographs for about two hours. But they've been repressed for so long that they're bound to react like that."

They then travelled to Brazil for eight more concerts. Robert told one magazine: "The concerts in Brazil were brilliant - just like a carnival. Whereas Argentina was wild in a football way, this was wild in a fun way. There were 12,000 people dancing all the time, even when we weren't playing! They have these weird things there called 'darks'. The darks are into punk - Siouxsie, Echo & The Bunnymen - and they're really funny. They do the top half properly, trying to get their hair right and wearing a black shirt, but then you look down and they've got Bermuda shorts and flip flops on! But at least they're trying."

The band returned to Britain, after a particularly unpleasant flight, jet-lagged but triumphant.

April proved to be a busy month for The Cure. On 10th 'Why Can't I Be You?'/'A Japanese Dream' was released, along with Pope's promo video, making No.21 in the charts. On 23rd, the Gala Premier of 'The Cure In Orange' - Pope's feature-length film of The Cure live - was held at the Odeon, Marble Arch. One reviewer of the film stated: "Despite their wobbly double chins and the fact that Simon Gallup is a deadringer for Mary in 'Eastenders', the band put in a sobering 23-song performance including spot-on renditions of all the singles from 'Boys Don't Cry' to 'Close To Me'. And Robert Smith even smiles (once). Could this

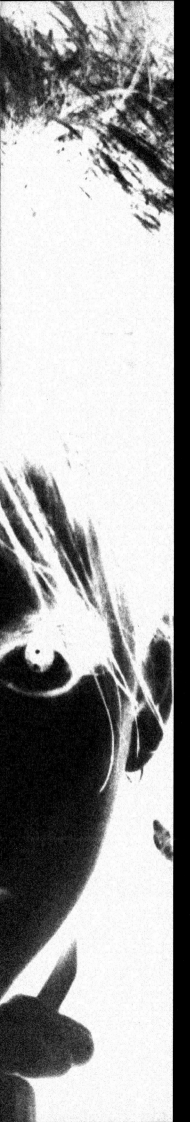

be due to the start of a new acting career? 'Strangely enough', says Robert, 'I've been offered a film role playing opposite Natassja Kinski in the last two days. But I turned it down. She's not my sort of woman.'"

Amongst this flurry of activity, the band themselves were on a promotional TV tour of Europe and, performed 'Why Can't I Be You?' and 'Catch' live on the last edition of The Tube.

On 22nd May the double album 'Kiss Me Kiss Me Kiss Me' was released and steamed into the UK album charts at No.6. It also reached No.35 in the American charts. The album received rave reviews from a world-wide press and, once again, hundreds of magazine covers were adorned with, what seemed like, an over-abundance of Robert's facial features. It is probable that Robert Smith is a strong contender for the 'man who has appeared on more Melody Maker covers' competition. He was everywhere, with each publication struggling to come up with a new angle - some previously untapped source of inspiration perhaps, or desperately extracting pearls of wisdom from the prolific Mr Smith. No subject was left uncovered, no stone left unturned.

Some of the more banal questions went like this: Do you own a teddy bear? "Yes. It was given to me on the day I was born. It's soaked with tears."

Why are you so scruffy?: "I don't have much time to be domestic. I've got an iron. I've never used it. My clothes dry like this, they just dry crinkled."

What's the first thing you do when you get up? "I wash my face with cold water and then I go and sit down with a cup of coffee and try to remember what I was dreaming about. I used to write them down - these days I usually discuss their more sordid aspects with Mary."

Would you like to swop places with Prince Charles? "No. I would have hated to be born into the Royal Family. It's a cushy number compared to a tramp, I suppose, but it has serious disadvantages. I hate any extreme - that's why I wouldn't like to be a real pop star and really famous; you're better in the happy medium. The Royal Family are laughable."

Do you like being rich? "When I feel I've got too much money I tend to give it away to charities and things. I have a weird sense of ethics - I don't think anybody should have lots of things. About four or five years ago I threw everything away because I'd started to hoard silly things like beer mats from a good night out. If you've got to run out in the middle of the night because the house is on fire the only thing you should really take is your teddy bear."

And so it went on. Everything the conscientious fan wanted to know about Robert Smith, Chameleon King of Rock.

In more serious interviews Robert explained the idea behind the cover of the album which depicted a close up of a pair of lips: "It was really the desire to swallow people. The idea of drowning them rather than kissing them." Commenting on the album he said: "It sounds more real than 'The Head On The Door'. That was a very constructed album. I sort of sacrificed any inspiration that could have come out of the five-piece for the sake of getting the record done because there were so

THE BRITS 1991 in conjunction BBC RADIO with

THE GREAT BRIT
USIC WEEKEN

WEMBLE
ARENA

FRIDAY 18th JANUA

Happy Mondays
James
The Farm
808 State
Northside
Candyland
Plus Personal Appearance
Beats International and

SATURDAY 19th JAN

The Cure
The Wedding Presen
New Model Army
Jesus Jones
The La's
Ride
Plus Personal Appearan
to be confirmed

SUNDAY 20th JANU

Ozzy Osbourne
Quireboys
Thunder
Magnum
Little Angels
Wolfsbane
Plus Special Guest Appea
David Coverdale
Tickets: £12.50 (each d

many things to be done after it. It's relaxed in that it's sure."

In July 'Catch'/'Breathe' was lifted from the album and released as a single, peaking at No.27 in the UK charts. The Pope-directed video has the band "moping about on patios overlooking the sea."

Robert told Doug Admission: "We would never have had this longevity if we'd had chart success a few year ago, because we'd have been too easily labelled. Now we're able to deal with it; we're much more slippery. We can escape tags and things because I'm used to playing the extremely foolish games that you have to indulge in.

"I never think 'Oh, grief, we're not in the Top Ten', because I look at the Top Ten and I'd seriously rather hang myself than be there if I had to be like the people that are in the Top Ten. I'd rather have a smaller audience that we meant more to, than a big audience we meant nothing to. That's a part of my nature, which is why we've always been slightly outside of the mainstream. Even if we sold ten million records I still don't think we'd ever be accepted as a mainstream group."

Two months later, the single 'Just Like Heaven'/'Snow In Summer' was released reaching No.29 in the UK charts and, in October, Robert described the accompanying video as: "A serious video. This is my favourite song on the 'Kiss Me' LP. It takes two incidents from real life: the main one happened where it was filmed, on Beachy Head, fifteen years earlier. The song's about hyperventilating - kissing and fainting to the floor. Mary dances with me in the video because she was the girl on Beachy Head, so it had to be her. In the song she goes over the edge and disappears: poetic licence. The idea is that one night like that is worth a thousand hours of drudgery."

obert spent two weeks on the South Dublin coast at this time and told Melody Maker's Steve Sutherland: "I'd go out by the sea each morning and sit down by the rocks. When I was younger it used to feel really, I don't know, I used to feel...inspired. And this time I actually felt really...dead."

The Cure embarked on a European tour in October. The band had expanded and had become a six-piece, due to the recruitment of former Psychedelic Fur keyboard player, Roger O'Donnell. He was chosen by Robert because he was "suitably mad" and came highly recommended by Boris Williams with whom he had played when they were both in The Thompson Twins' backing group.

The tour ended on 9th December after three sell-out nights at Britain's Wembley Arena. Sam King wrote a rather odd review of one of the Wembley shows: "Everything about them, especially now, suggest a massive communal love-in with the ultimate aim of regressing beyond the red veined womb of innocence into a prenatal state of total pleasure. The Cure reflect Robert's unholy ultrasexuality. Each song, with the exception of the dour 'Faith' rejoices in the lithe axle-ground shower of eroticism. Each song satiates, devouring your insides, curdling your loins until you can't take it anymore and then does it all again. Childhood ends as pop's lust resurfaces. Lipsmackin'." One can only assume that she liked the show!

BOTTLE IN THE SEA

Hope

o coincide with the shows, Zomba published 'Ten Imaginary Years', the official Cure biography written by Robert with more than a little help from Steve Sutherland and Lydie Barbarian, a french journalist and a major Cure fan. All in all, 1987 had been a very satisfactory year.

In the New Year, The Cure took stock of their achievements. After eleven years and eight studio, one live and three compilation albums, they had sold over eight million albums world-wide, with 'Kiss Me Kiss Me Kiss Me' grossing over two million sales alone. The Cure were absolutely massive in France, but there was no market in the world in which they didn't enjoy a respectable presence. They received a royalty rate of 20% which is double that of most artists.

Robert granted Robert Sandall an interview and said: "I do have, um, this very strange split personality. I can reach a point where I am fanatically ordered. And at the other extreme I let everything go to pieces. Put myself at physical risk. Like when we were in Paris I climbed round the outside of the hotel we were in to get into one of the other rooms. On the second floor. And being in America changes my personality completely. It makes me monstrous. As loud and obnoxious as a lot of the people you meet over there are. I can't stand America. I mean the playing's all right, but the nutters there are worse than anywhere in the world."

He also gave another explanation for one of his visual trademarks, the smudged lipstick: "I started wearing it because it made me feel confident and more attractive. I'm completely featureless without it. But on stage I

always used to lean my mouth on the mike and shut my eyes so I wouldn't have to see the people. And at the end I'd come off with lipstick smeared all over my face, so I thought I might as well go on with it like that and make it look intentional."

The Cure had the world at their feet but they had one problem which was rapidly becoming insurmountable - Lol's drinking. Robert disclosed later to Rolling Stone that matters had come to a head during their 1987 tour. "Lol just drank his way through the tour to such a degree that he didn't bother retaliating. It was like watching some kind of handicapped child being constantly poked with a stick." Once again, Robert pleaded with him to shape up and told him that it would be his final warning. Lol promised to do better.

In February 'Hot Hot Hot!!!' was released as a single but, despite rave reviews, only made No.45 in the UK charts, primarily due to Pope's brilliant but unacceptable video, nicknamed 'Midgets In Sunglasses'. Robert told Select: "This was about three strange sexual experiences: in the basement of a club, on a ferry and at home in my bedroom. Lightning striking was an analogy. I was thinking of a children's book - Earthfast (by William Mayne) about a boy hit by lightning and going back in time - and of that bloke in the Guinness Book Of Records who's been hit numerous times. I told Tim Pope I wanted us to look like a lowdown funky soul band. He translated 'lowdown' as 'dwarf' and 'soul band' as 'black-and-white'. Polydor said it wouldn't get shown. It didn't."

In August 13th, Robert finally did the

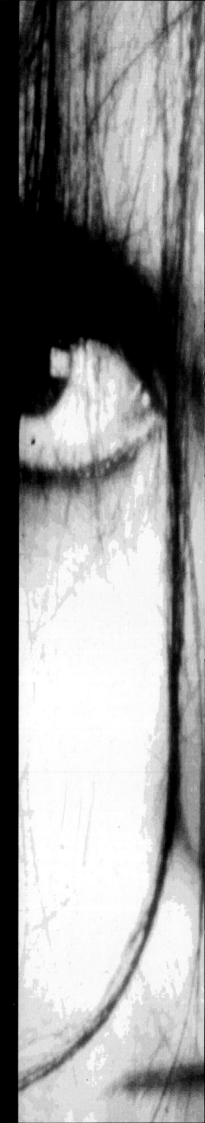

honourable thing and married Mary at
the Benedictine Monastery in Worth
Abbey in Sussex. All the band
members turned out for the occasion
with Simon as Best Man. The wedding
was a well-kept secret, Robert
preferring to marry his childhood
sweetheart away from the glare of the
media spotlight. He told the NME's
James Brown: "No one knew the
venue. Everyone had to get on a coach
and be taken there in secret. Some
people thought we'd gone a bit over the
top but the wedding had nothing to do
with the group and I wanted it
emphasised that it was about me and
Mary. If just one journalist or one bunch
of fans had been there it would have
ruined it for both of us and both sets of
parents."

obert's answer to a question by
Brad Balfour on the possibility
of having children was: "I've
thought about it from time to time but
it's too much responsibility - I'm too
erratic to be a father. I really love kids;
the happiest times of my life are spent
with kids. I've got six nephews and I
constantly try to teach them the finer
arts of football. But I think my attitude
towards them would be different if I
were actually the father. Like my older
brother owns three of them. I see his
attitude when he feels responsible for
them and he gets very nervous
thinking, my God are they going to kill
themselves? Whereas I just join in on
their level. If they scream, I scream
back; if they nip me, I nip back.
Consequently, they treat me as one of
their own. Ultimately, though, it's up to
Mary. If she decides she wants children
then it would be different."

Robert and Mary invested in a house
on the coast as a retreat from the
rigours of his rock 'n' roll lifestyle.

Robert commented: "Well, now I've got a house on the beach - actually it's not a beach with sand, but pebbles - and I can look out the window towards the sea, maybe such a peaceful environment will rekindle my paternal instinct. But I doubt it."

he NME noted other reasons behind the move: "Robert Smith detests the dirt and noise of London and no longer considers it safe to walk the streets at the wrong end of the day. He doesn't consider himself famous, and it's because the freedom of the country and not the intrusion of fans that he plans to move away from the capital."

One publication quoted Robert replying to the question that marriage had tamed him: "No. It's no different. I mean, I was always domesticated. I love cooking. I'm a brilliant cook. I can't help thinking about weird things when I cook, then I suddenly realise I've poured sixteen squillion pints too much milk into something! But I hate cooking for lots of people because it seems really pointless - just cooking it all and then someone sits and eats it.."

In December, the band reassembled at Boris Williams' West Country house to work on some songs for their new album. He explained in Time Out : "After the whole 'Kiss Me' thing I took a break for a couple of months to escape "the group" and I started pooling together all the work I'd written for some imaginary solo project I keep meaning to do. When it was ready I decided to try some of it out with the band and once we started working on it, it was becoming obvious we should record another Cure album. We carried the mood over even though those songs are still there waiting for this solo

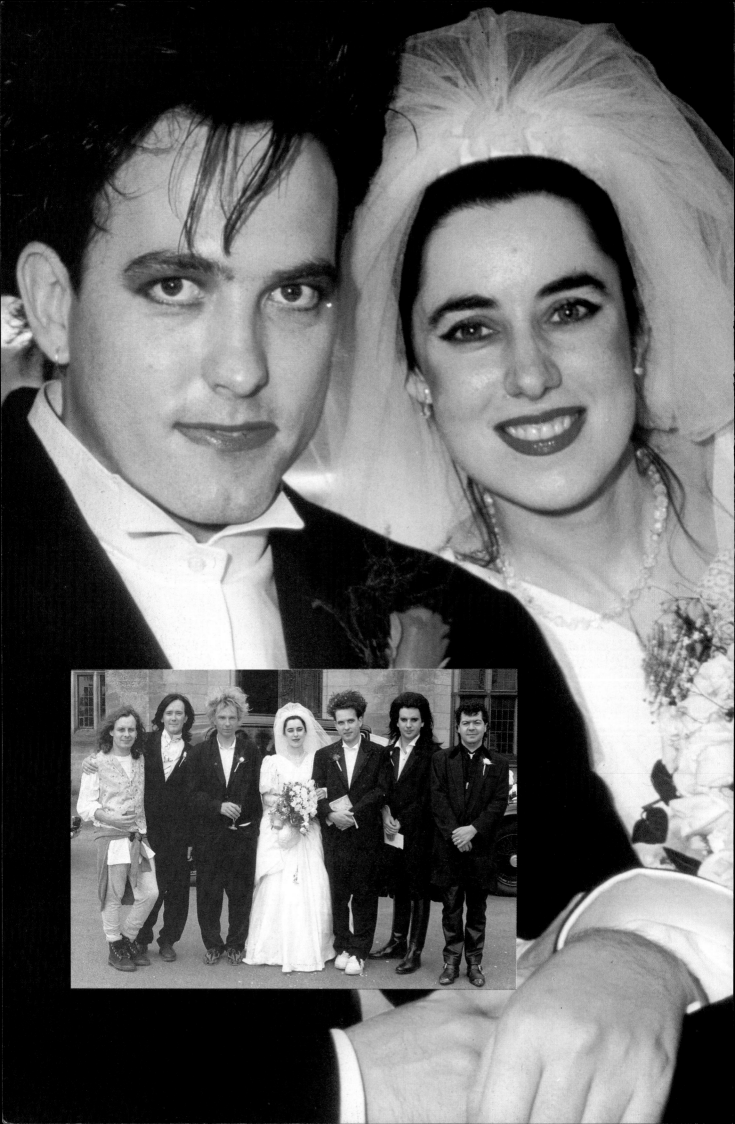

album to materialise. This time I just felt more comfortable with a low-key atmosphere and I think everybody else just slid down into it too.

"I wanted to utilise the time you're allowed with a CD. I wanted to be able to stretch an idea over an hour and keep a theme running through it and take time building up emotion without having to worry about the constraints of twenty minutes a side. It's still broken up with lighter songs to keep it from being turgid, but concentrates on one aspect of The Cure's music to generate some emotion back into the band."

The majority of the album was recorded on a forty-eight track desk at Outside Studios, then remixed at RAK. The decision to go from twenty-four to forty-eight track was explained by co-producer Dave Allen in International Musician: "Well, we wanted to make it bigger and give ourselves somewhere to go, technically-speaking. I think you can make better records with forty-eight track, because if you get an idea and you want to try it out, you just go and do it. You don't have to worry about using up tracks because you've got plenty to work with."

The resulting album was entitled 'Disintegration' and included the tracks: 'Plainsong', 'Pictures Of You', 'Closedown', 'Love Song', 'Last Dance', 'Lullaby', 'Fascination Street', 'Prayers', 'For Rain', 'The Same Deep Water As You', 'Disintegration', 'Homesick' and 'Untitled'. The album was scheduled for release on May 2nd, 1989, and featured Robert's most intense and agonized work for several years.

During the recording of 'Disintegration' Robert decided that he could no longer

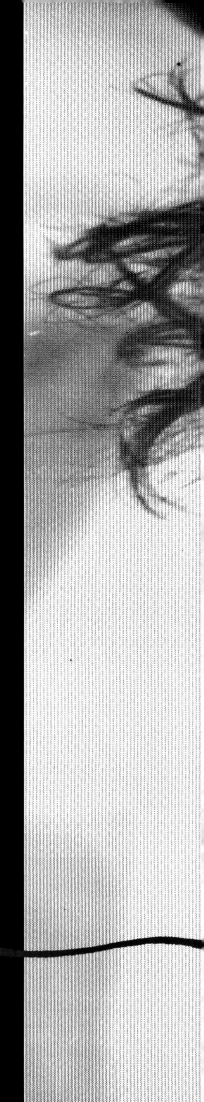

tolerate Lol's inebriated presence in the band and, shortly after the album was completed, he discussed getting rid of Lol with the others. Porl stated that he wouldn't be prepared to tour if Lol stayed, while Simon went so far to say that he would leave the band if Lol didn't! Robert told Select later: "All through, I always papered over the cracks and felt a genuine sympathy for him, until it reached the point where he was just taking the piss, literally. During 'Disintegration' he didn't once set foot in the studio. That's fact. He went there so he was physically in the building, so that he could pick up his paycheck.

"If you sat him down in front of a keyboard I doubt if he could reel off more than about two Cure songs. And one of them would be 'A Forest', and that's because it's embedded in his mind because we laughed at him for so many years, because we had this tape of what he sounded like onstage playing the first four notes really out of time."

The last time Robert ever saw Lol was at the party to celebrate the completion of 'Disintegration' held just before Christmas 1988 at RAK studios. It was an ugly scene. Robert takes up the story: "He slagged off everything to do with the album, the group and me, and just got drunker and drunker. He said the album was shit, because he hadn't played on any of the songs. It was the first time he'd heard them, I think, and he didn't like them - but he was still prepared to take his money and go on tour and suffer it."

obert explained in an interview with Q: "I just told him that I didn't want him around any more. He'd become a fixture, only appearing at mealtimes and totally out

of his head. Lol's never had any musical input and he's the only one of us who hasn't been able to pull back from the excesses of being in the group. His function has always been as a sort of victim, and by the end of all the jokes, the bitterness, the conversation everything was focusing on him rather than on the music."

Robert wrote to Lol a few days later and explained his reasons for not wanting him in the band any longer. He never got any response.

 hile Robert was busy giving press conferences explaining the reasons for Lol's departure from the band, Lol himself retreated to his house in Devon to try to come to terms with what had happened. He kept silent on the subject of his unceremonious sacking until two years later, when he gave interviews for the first time whilst promoting his new band, Presence. He told the NME's Roger Morton: "Well, I hadn't been happy for a very long time, and I wasn't...I wasn't very well. I was drinking far too much, but that's really like a symptom, not the cause of anything...It's one of those things where it's so involved. The Cure's so much like a family and very incestuous, that it's really hard to work out why you don't talk to your Uncle Jack any more."

When asked if he felt that Robert was a particularly unreasonable person he replied: "Sometimes he can be. At that stage I

ANIMAL

CATS & APES

people around him would pander to
that. I think maybe one of the reasons
he felt uncomfortable with me is that I
knew all our past, and the silly things
we'd done...and perhaps he didn't want
to be reminded of it, or his past life."

I n the New Year, press releases
were sent to the media
heralding the release of a
single from the album, 'Lullaby'/'Babble'
in April, followed by the album
'Disintegration' in May and news of a
world tour which would kick off in June
at The Glastonbury Festival, refuting
the speculation that The Cure had
retired from the live scene.

"Lullaby'/'Babble' was duly released
and rapidly became a smash hit,
reaching No.5 in the UK charts, the
highest position achieved by the band
to this date. The press loved the single
and one review stated: "Superficially a
subtle, poppy sedative, 'Lullaby' is
really a psychotic dreamscape that
revels in a surreal Daliesque logic.
Here, deep within Smith's nocturnal
reverie, the Spiderman does battle with
the shivering victims of the Sleepman,
repeating an eternal childhood
nightmare - sucking eyes, pulling flesh,
twisting the psyche, until all that's left is
a frightened clammy youth.

"Disorientating in the same way that
the Buttholes' 'Kuntz' is, 'Lullaby' is as
sinister as its title is comforting,
recalling the spectres of the child
catcher from 'Chitty Chitty Bang Bang',
the Texas Chainsaw murderer and the
meandering footsteps you're sure you
hear in the dark, late at night. God only
knows what Smith sees when his eyes
are closed but it's odds on that it's not

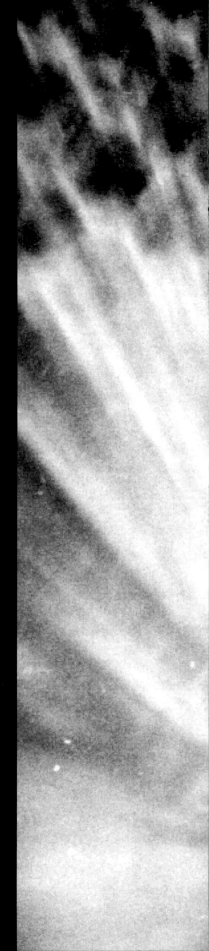

physically attractive. This, on the other hand, is almost classic."

The single was accompanied by an award-winning Pope video in which Robert lies in bed, covered in cobwebs and is devoured whole by a giant spider. He told Melody Maker: "It was like a dream...no, not really a dream, just something that used to bother me a lot as a kid so I knew exactly what I wanted it to look like."

Robert told Select: "I actually drew in boxes what I wanted the video to look like. We did it in a kind of Christopher Lee way. I refused to have the real spider on me: they had a bloke there with an antidote and I tried but I couldn't. It was kind of a throwaway video - Jim Kerr didn't understand it, my nephews did. Given the choice of audience I'd rather have my nephews."

The success of the single meant the inevitable appearance on Top Of The Pops. The video was deemed too harrowing for early-evening television so the band had to perform the song themselves. It proved to be a trying day for The Cure.

hey were scheduled to appear sandwiched between Diana Ross and Debbie Gibson, in itself a concept that they found less than rivetting. After seemingly endless waiting and rehearsals they were informed by a BBC official that the producer had decided that Robert's look of kohl lined eyes and smeared lipstick would be a bad influence on the nation's kids and refused to allow the band to play until the offending powder and paste was removed. Robert was absolutely furious and the band marched back to their dressing room, refusing to compromise. Left with the

prospect of their scheduling being
disrupted at short notice, the BBC
eventually gave in and Robert, after his
anger had abated told Melody Maker
with a smile: "At least we still threaten
people. That has to be a good thing."

In May, 'Disintegration' was launched
with all the usual furore associated with
a release from a band of The Cure's
internationally successful status. Once
again, Robert's face seemed to be
everywhere. No publication was
complete without the obligatory Robert
Smith interview and fans were busy
rearranging their holidays to fit in with
the forthcoming tour. The album went
straight into the UK charts at N.3
amidst rapturous press accolades.

Carole Linfield wrote: "So is
'Disintegration' aptly named? Ironically,
typically, no, since, if anything, it's a
return to roots and a fundamental
display of everything that The Cure do
best. It's grainy, growing music in which
Smith's moaning vocals often take
something of a back seat, allowing the
atmosphere to swirl and surround."

Another reviewer stated: "The Cure's
'Disintegration' is a milestone in pop
history, marking the spot where New
Wave clearly ceased to be new. Twelve
years after he began depressing
people, singer-songwriter Robert Smith
became a star. The band can now
boast two legitimate hit singles,
'Fascination Street' and 'Love Song' as
well as a massive global tour during
which the Cure surpassed Pink Floyd in
the highly competitive field of glum
spectacles. Never before had so many
people enjoyed having so little fun at a
rock show. But the album's title may be
prophetic; Smith vowed that this will be
The Cure's last album."

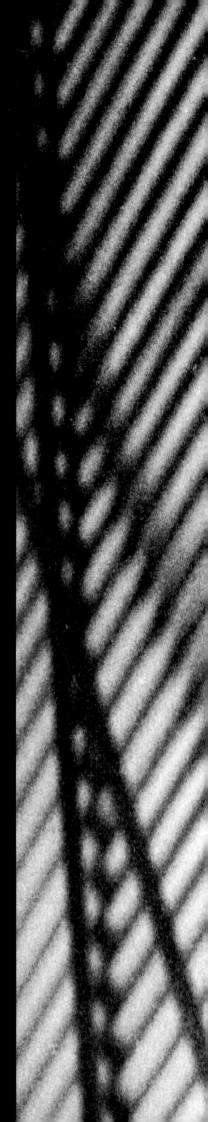

Lime Lizard, naming 'Disintegration' as 'Album Of The Month...Year???' wrote: "'Disintegration' is seemly created in the same doomy atmosphere as 'Seventeen Seconds', 'Faith' and 'Pornography', however, it's different. It's missing the I-have-slit-my-wrists-now-let-me-lie-in-peace attitude. It's a triumphant cry of the underdog after winning a long and bloody battle. Smith pours out his pure and deepened emotions like a stream of nethering mist. But it doesn't seem to be for us. Are we peering into private and intimate works which were undoubtedly snatched from Smith's spiderweb-laced bedroom?"

On a more negative note, Chris Roberts felt: "'Disintegration' isn't the most depressing record I've heard recently. That would be the Simple Minds album, which is depressing because it's so terribly, terribly bad. But 'Disintegration' is at least as mollifying as waking up in Rumania in winter with no clothes on. It's about as much fun as losing a limb. It's as life-affirming as chopping down a tree and stamping on the squirrels. It's as sobering as seeing The Cure play live, which in recent years has become an increasingly agonising experience."

Robert responded to the accusation that The Cure were depressing by saying: "The people who call us depressing are either remembering the 'Faith'/'Pornography' period, or they never listen to our music. We're too stylistically varied, too kaleidoscopic to be called depressing. Of course we've been involved in tours and records that have been depressing, but it's not an attitude. When we're on stage it's usually elating, it excuses the mundaneness of the previous twenty-two hours. I can forget that maybe eighteen hours ago I was throwing up over a balcony."

The Cure embarked on 'The Prayer Tour' as 'Disintegration' thundered into the American charts at No.12. Kicking off In Copenhagen, they played dates throughout Scandinavia and then moved on to Germany. On 13th May they headlined the Bizarre Festival in Lorelei, West Germany, supported by The Mission, The Sugarcubes, The Pixies, Shelleyan Orphan and Eat. Simon Wlliams of the NME witnessed the The Cure's performance and liked what he saw: "By statistical definition, The Cure are stadium rockers, whoppingly huge across the Continent. Yet they have avoided the requisite mannerisms for such enormous arenas. There's no scaling of scaffolding, no impassioned speeches about the fourth world, nor any banner-waving bollocks.

"Sure the tour trappings - the lightshow and super-productive smoke machine - are there, because they have to be. But Robert Smith refuses to pander to the pop star game, and his colleagues (Simon Gallup's Hooky-like bassplaying aside) barely twitch throughout the set. By not forcing themselves on the audience or patronising their followers, The Cure prevent themselves from becoming sitting ducks, grinning inanely as the cynics spit lead.

"Ah, the highlights. The pinnacles of perfection. The frenzied reaction to 'The Walk', twenty thousand continentals stung into action by THAT maddening keyboard riff. It becomes inordinately difficult to avoid trundling out the cliches. 'Boys Don't Cry' is nigh on awesome - I'm convinced it's going to raise the roof until I realise there isn't one. Phew. It should, by rights, be the

farewell, enabling The Cure to vanish on a helium-stoked high. But such is Smith's perverse wont they return for the post-climax of 'Faith', sending the evening off on a subbonly low-key note without so much as a bedtime story."

The Cure were going down well everywhere with both the press and audiences. Off-stage, however, stories of drunken binges and all manner of various capers began to circulate.

After the festival in Lorelei, both The Cure and The Mission were rumoured to have had a drinking competition resulting in total oblivion for all concerned. The Mission's Wayne Hussey, however, was claiming victory. Robert told Steve Sutherland: "God bless him. We left him in the middle of this square, kind of spinning round slowly, wondering if he was in the right town. I got on well with him which was quite surprising - well, y'know, since I'd met him before. The Pixies were really nice as well and I liked Einer from The Sugarcubes. When I first went up to him, I thought 'Oh, we're gonna have a ruck here', because straight away there was that kind of friction. But, after about fifteen minutes, we were like old buddies."

The tour continued through Germany, taking in Switzerland, Austria and Greece. They also toured Eastern Europe for the first time. Robert told Sutherland: "It made a real difference going to Yugoslavia and Hungary because that was the point. After about four weeks, the tour would have started to get a bit stale and you'd know the reaction of the audience and what's going to happen. But, in Eastern Europe, we didn't really know what response would occur and we played a lot of old stuff. Their reaction was quite bizarre because they knew all the words to the songs. We've never had a penny in royalties from Hungary, so I assumed we didn't sell any records there and yet the entire audience was singing along to every song. It was weird - I just kept stopping and laughing because it was like phonetics, y'know, they couldn't have understood what they were singing."

 rom the Eastern Bloc they toured Greece, Italy and Spain eventually reaching France where The Cure's popularity had reached epic proportions. Sounds' journalist Keith Cameron joined the band in Paris and Robert, again, suggested that the current tour would be their last. "That's probably why I've enjoyed it this time. I'm so set that, when we come back from America, that's it, that I know nothing in the world can change my mind this time. So each night when we're onstage I know we've got...I think it's thirty-one concerts left now, seventy-four hours left. I'm actually counting down and each one gets progressively better because everyone's beginning to realise that I do mean it, and it gives a real edge to the performances."

Robert light-heartedly told another reporter in Paris: "Most of the entourage have taken the pace quite well. Only one of the roadies had to go home due to terminal boredom which is quite good by our standards! And Boris, the drummer, took a short holiday during Simon Gallup's bass solo, but apart from that we've managed to stick together. We've had the girlfriends along too - they've been making us sandwiches and generally lending an air of sanity to the proceedings, ha ha ha."

DESTINY

Cure to tour no more

★ ROBERT SMITH says the current US tour by THE CURE will be the group's last. "It's reached a stage where I personally can't cope with it, so I've decided this is the last time we're gonna tour," Smith says. "It's no big deal. I just don't feel comfortable anymore with the kind of attention that I'm getting. It's purely the numbers of people that want a bit of The Cure or want a bit of me."

Smith complains he can't go for a walk in Europe. "We were in some of the most beautiful cities in Europe, and I couldn't go out without having an entourage," he says. "I tried a disguise and it didn't work. I had no make-up and my hair flat and a hat on, but people recognized me, and when I asked them how they knew it was me they said it was my shoes, so the second time I did it I changed my shoes, and I was still recognized."

CHANCE
SLEEP
OBLIVION

THE CUR

THE CURE

THE CURE AVEC

GUEST : SHELLEYAN ORPHAN

12 JUIN	COLMAR	3 JUILLET	BORDEAUX
13 JUIN	LYON	4 JUILLET	NANTES
14 JUIN	GRENOBLE	5 JUILLET	BREST
16 JUIN	FREJUS	7 JUILLET	CAEN
JUIN	ARLES	11 JUILLET	REIMS

LET ____ **PARIS-BERCY 20 H**

UVEL ALBUM : **DISINTEGRATION**

LOCATION PARIS : FNAC - POPB - VIRGIN MEGASTORE - PROVINCE : POINTS
DE VENTE HABITUELS SUR MINITEL 36.15 CODE NRJ. CLUB.
INFOS CONCERT SUR MINITEL 36.15 CODE NRJ.

La plus belle ra

RECITAL
Rock & Pop

AGram

THE CURE

VENTA DE ENTRADAS
musimundo

ESTADIO FERRO

17 · 18 MARZO

NO HABRA ENTRADAS DE FAVOR

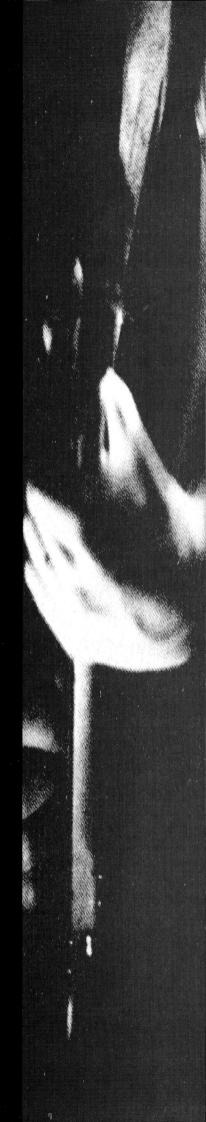

From France, they visited Dublin, played a gig in Birmingham and Glasgow and returned to London, ending the European leg of the tour with three nights at Wembley Arena. All three shows were recorded for a possible release in 1990.

an Gittins reviewed one of the shows: "It's a huge show, the lights are glorious, and yet The Cure are never showbiz. They've no theatre like Price or The Pet Shop Boys. Rather, they shuffle on stage, pale, awkward figures, and huddle there, playing these clever, silver slivers of music. What they do is absurdly flimsy, tenuous, yet always held together by Smith's provocative, mischievous imagination, the daft fairy tales he dreams up. The Cure make fancies into songs for no reason at all, and it shows. The new LP is hard to love. But tonight they're flying.

"The Cure win over Wembley because they're still near and intimate. Fitful and fickle. Unlike the Minds, who spell out the truth in huge capitals, they're shadows, angles and imponderables. We can't tell where they're coming from. And it's typical that, after turning all of Wembley into one demented, spindly dance for 'Boys Don't Cry', they return for a grim, interminable encore ending with 'Faith', stubborn monochrome guitar like water torture. The Cure are still hard work. And they leave us not with a kiss, but a frown. Perverse buggers! So - a shock! - one of the best shows I've seen this year. The Cure are still around, and it's no great sin. They turned Wembley on its head. This was precious. Kiss them, kiss them, kiss them. The Cure roll on."

After a short break, it was time to travel

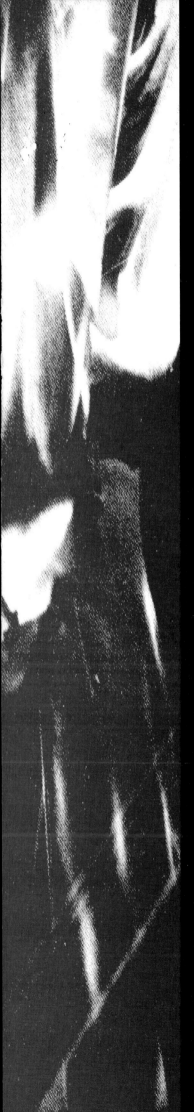

to America to complete the last leg of the tour. Robert, who had always hated flying, decided that, on this occasion, the band would sail to America on board the QE2. At the same time, the single 'Love Song'/'2 Late' was released, giving the band another Top Ten hit by reaching No.8 in the UK charts. One reviewer wrote: "'Love Song' isn't their best but it can hardly be described as pompous. It's very ethereal and breezy, like an afterthought on one of Kate Bush's very private shopping lists."

he Cure kicked off their American tour at the Giants Stadium in New Jersey. Rolling Stone commented: "Had somebody predicted in 1978 that 49,223 people in a stadium would one day clap and sing along as the Gothic rockers in The Cure played '10.15 Saturday Night', that person would have been considered a ripe candidate for the loony bin. But that's just what happened at Giants Stadium on this balmy August night - people danced, sang and what can only be described as a good time as The Cure played some of pop's most melancholy music.

'Love Song' was released in America whilst the band were touring there and shot straight into the No.2 slot, and was only kept from achieving No.1 status by Janet Jackson's 'Miss You Much'. The Cure had finally triumphed over that most elusive, yet lucrative, of territories, America.

The American tour ended on 23rd September and the band returned to Britain for a well-deserved rest.

The greatest of years for The Cure, 1989 was rounded off by the band cleaning up in The Melody Maker

Awards Poll. 'Disintegration' was voted Album Of The Year by Melody Maker's writers and 'Lullaby' came fourth in the Top Single category. To mark the occasion, Melody Maker asked Robert to highlight his most memorable moments of the past year and past decade.

THE BEST THINGS ABOUT THE EIGHTIES WERE?

"Solidarity. The Rise of anti-nuclear feeling. The dawning realisation that pollution isn't someone else's problem. The Sky at Miraval. Giving up flying. The Soviets leaving Afghanistan. All the Voyager space flight discoveries. Computer adventure games. Ensoniq Mirage. 'Tess'. Daley Thompson. Most of New Order's 12-inch singles. All of Kate Bush. 'E.T.' 'Comic Strip'/'Young Ones'. Liverpool beating Roma final. Mike Tyson. Lech Walesa. 'Time Bandits'. 'Brazil'. Brazil. Mother Teresa. Getting married. 'Paris, Texas'. Paris, France. Tokyo. 'Blue Velvet'. Viz. Frank at the Westbury. Dublin. 'Dare'. 'Sign O The Times'. Ian Botham. Peter Ustinov. Disneyland. 'King Of Comedy'. 'Raging Bull'. 'Closer'. Watching Charles & Di from San Francisco. 'Grey Gardens' documentary. 'The Glove'. Seedy clubs. Cocteau Twins. Bunnymen. 'Chainsaw Arms'. Being in The Cure. Surviving..."

THE WORST THINGS ABOUT THE EIGHTIES WERE?

"The continuing regimes of persecution round the world. The Soviets in Afghanistan. The Troubles in Northern Ireland. Plane crashes. Famine. Iraq/Iran conflict. The Space Shuttle disaster. Rupert Murdoch and Robert Maxwell's growing media control. SDI

(Star Wars). Wheel Clamps. The rampant ego-mania of mundane characters as diverse as Scargill, Morrissey, Gadaffi, Thatcher, Gillick and either Pet Shop tosser. AIDS. London. The Falkland's War. Tiananmen Square. Heysel Stadium. Maradonna's 'Hand Of God'. Sandox Rhine pollution disaster. All pollution. 'The Storm'. Losing sixpences, red telephone boxes and one second in 1988. Not losing Dusty Springfield, Billy Joel, Bobby Robson and many others. Losing Satre, Hitchcock, Sellers, Cooper, McQueen, Lennon, Koesstler. Bunuel, Miro, Du Pri, Borges, Genet, Chagall, Curtis, Burton and too many others to think about."

During the beginning of 1990, The Cure laid low. A further single was released from the 'Disintegration' album, entitled 'Pictures Of You'/'Last Dance' on April 14th which entered the UK charts at No.24. Tim Pope's inevitable video accompanied the release and featured the band playing in a snowscape surrounded by palm trees. Robert told Select: "I lost the pictures I always carried around in my wallet. I realised that I'm clutching old pictures of things, even taken before my birth, to give me a sense that things went on then. After spending a lot building the 'Love Song' set we just took three Super-8 cameras to the place I thought it should look like. I wanted a sunny feel, but it mentions snow in the words. Snow looks like sand in black-and-white, so I thought, Let's start as if it's in the sun, then pull away and you'll see a blizzard. The old adage 'The camera doesn't lie' isn't true."

Music Week reviewed the single: "Third track to be released from 'Disintegration', and just as powerful as

'Lullaby' and 'Love Song'. No great surprises for non-converts, though. The guitar lines and tortured vocal are unmistakably Cure, but they have enough diehard fans to run out an buy it for the live B-sides to chalk up yet another hit."

owever, one reviewer wrote: "Magical bass, purchased mail-order from the Joy Division back catalogue, I wouldn't wonder. 'Pictures Of You' is another mournful Smith lament (what else can you do with a voice like his?) singing about photos and memories, long distance love affairs and delicacy. Like any sensible crooner should. Straight up: this is so much 'Everything's Gone Green' - era New Order, it could provoke lawsuits, or at least flashed accusations across darkened rooms - billowing and breaking hearts along the way."

There were no lawsuits and, at around the same time, The Cure announced they would headline the Glastonbury Festival on June 23rd. as well as appear at a handful of European festivals in the summer. The other dates included were Roskilde in Denmark, Laysin in Switzerland, Tourhout and Werchter in Belgium. This news was received with delight by both the press and fans alike who feared that Robert's unofficial announcement of The Cure's retirement the previous year could have marked the end of their live career.

A few weeks later, the news was leaked that The Cure had also agreed to headline at a special all-day gig at Crystal Palace on August 11th. The Garden Party was to be the first for a decade. The original Garden Parties were the biggest open air concerts of

194

the Seventies featuring such luminaries
as Pink Floyd and the Faces. This
news put paid to the 'No more Cure'
speculation for once and for all.

In an interview with Sounds'
scribe Ethlie Ann Vare later in
the year, Robert denied that he
had said The Cure were going to quit
touring: "When we were in America last
year, the concerts we played at the end
of September a year ago, very soon
after that there was a lot of conflict
within the group just on that tour - the
concerts were brilliant, but the
problems with touring have always
been there. Because of the way the
group is, because of the type of songs
we play and the make up within the
group, it generally leads to a kind of
excess on tour.

"Not excess in the rock 'n' roll sense,
but the feeling that you're there not
only to perform as well as you can, as
it's going to be your last concert, but
also to experience everything as if it's
your last day on earth It tends to
become very emotionally and
physically exhausting. And as I get
older, I find it takes me longer to
recover.

"I never at any point said we weren't
playing live again, which people keep
saying I did but I'm quite sure that I
didn't. Because going away for a
couple of weeks and playing five or six
concerts is very different mentally to
packing your bag and leaving home for
three months."

To prepare for the forthcoming dates,
The Cure retreated to the Berkshire
countryside to rehearse. Melody
Maker's Steve Sutherland joined them
there and asked the reason for their re-
emergence in 1990. Porl told him "I

think he just missed playing. He hasn't said too much about it and really we haven't made it too much of a deal." Simon backed him up by stating "The old bastard just wanted to do it again."

Robert's explanation was that he wanted to work on some new material and the Festival season in Europe provided him with the opportunity of doing just that. He told Sutherland: "Everyone's too pissed or out of it by the time we go on to notice what we're like. It's great."

Just prior to leaving for their first, unannounced, festival in France, Roger O'Donnell quit the band. The exact reason for his departure are unclear but it appears to have had something to do with an argument over money. Perry Bamonte, The Cure's long-standing guitar technician, had been drafted in to replace him. Perry explained later: "Back when I started with The Cure, they needed someone to be a guitar tech, but I'd usually end up doing all kinds of things. I still haven't really had time to put into words what it feels like to be onstage with them. When we were in Paris we did this concert outdoors, and it was my first time playing live with them. It was an unannounced show - people found out about it only a couple of hours before we went on. That was the best thing for me, because it wasn't like going and having the hall filled up with Cure fans - that would have been more nerve racking."

On 23rd June, The Cure headlined The Glastonbury Festival. Their first British appearance in over a year was marred by the injury of a young fan, crushed at the front of the stage. One publication reported that the whole event was

extremely badly organised: "Other fans complained of being dragged out of cars and beaten up by gangs. Food and drink sellers at the site were told that, if they were wearing trader's passes, organisers couldn't guarantee their safety against thieves. Many people had their cars broken into or simply kicked in. The organisation backstage was no better. The whole area was over-populated with the result that several bands were mobbed by fans who'd managed to get behind the stage. Seasoned Glastonbury goers were in agreement that this was the worst organised festival ever.

"There was nearly a tragedy during the Cure's set on Saturday night when the crowd gathered around the stage became crushed against the security barrier. One girl at the front of the stage was rendered unconscious. Twenty year-old Sarah Besford was pulled out of the crowd and given the kiss of life by a security guard. A medic arrived a started pumping her chest. Within minutes more medics arrived on the scene and she was given electric shock treatment and put on a drip. A police helicopter was radioed. It landed stage right and the girl was flown to hospital. Luckily, she made a full recovery and was able to discharge herself the next day."

Oblivious to the near-disaster occurring in front of them, The Cure began to play a stunning set. Robert appeared extremely relaxed considering it was only Perry Bamonte's second gig with the band. The end with a new track that they

PARTY

ests

CE BOWL

AUGUST

0pm

ble from

nier, Albermarle,

d all usual agents

TLINES

4 / 081 741 8989

had recently recorded at The Farmyard Studios, 'Never Enough' According to one reviewer: "It sounds great - Smith's vocal precariously poised between self-pity and anger, the guitars ranging in a mad wah wah orgy. It's rough and ready and rises majestic above the chaos which pretty much sums up The Cure tonight."

Two months later, after tramping the Euro-festival circuit, The Cure returned to Britain for The Garden Party at The Crystal Palace Bowl. Again, they were in cracking form. Andrew Mueller for Melody Maker reviewed the gig: "The sun sets, the light show flickers and flashes into being, and we at last have something resembling atmosphere - though blue, red and pink washes of spotlight bouncing off water and through trees would be enough to lend Lloyd Cole with a banjo a certain wrenching poignancy. The Cure's stage now looks like a light at the end of the tunnel and people are dancing up and down the hills. The first encore ends with 'Charlotte Sometimes'. The second with 'Faith' dedicated to the supporters. The third goes 'Boys Don't Cry', '10.15 Saturday Night', 'Killing An Arab' and 'Never Enough'. Then the pond fills with fireworks, the top of the stage lights up, the band leave and Smith stands there, grinning hopelessly, taking it all in. Magnificent. There will always be a Cure. Long may they spring eternal."

In the early hours of Saturday, 1st September, The Cure had a crack at broadcasting to the citizens of London via their own pirate radio station - Cure FM. "Hold on London - we're just going to play some Jane's Addiction while we tune in the aerial" were the words that launched station on the airwaves of the capital. However, the whole event was

doomed to failure from the start.

In a hastily erected mock-up studio housed in Fiction's offices, the band, DJs, TV crews, journalists and record company staff collected to take part in this unique event which was due to be picked up by an audience of 10,000. Everyone waited with baited breath to witness the launch of the first band-run radio station when it was announced that the link between the studio and the transmitter, situated on top of a tower block somewhere in Maida Vale, wasn't connecting. Excuses of too much lead on the roof of the building abounded and the friendly neighbourhood pirate operators who set up the gear began to frantically rewire their home-made electronic boxes of tricks.

Many hours, and many bottles of beer later, the fault was finally detected and Cure FM was launched onto an unsuspecting public. The point of the exercise was to use the ruse of the radio station to enable Cure fans preview selections from the band's forthcoming 'Mixed Up' album before its scheduled October release date. Two top American DJs, Mike Halloran from 91X in San Diego and Lewis Largent from KROQ had been specially flown in to supervise the event. Brilliantly re-recorded versions of 'The Walk' and 'A Forest' were aired as well as a stunning remix of 'In Between Days'. One surprise of the night was the broadcast of a Cure cover of The Doors' classic 'Hello, I Love You' which they had recently recorded for the 40th Anniversary of their American record label, Elektra. The track was to be included in a special compilation album, marking the anniversary, entitled 'Rubaiyat'.

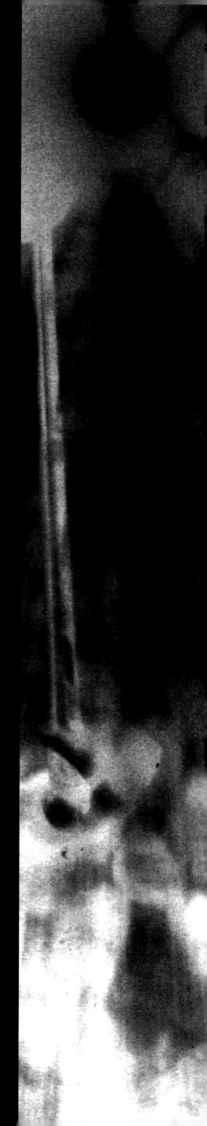

Just before dawn, Robert closed the station down by introducing the new single 'Never Enough' with the words: "This song is dedicated to the weeken - over which we're only going to get four hours sleep." Those who were sti awake drifted off into the night, including Robert and Mary, who disappeared into the back of a taxi.

Later in the month, on 17th Septembe 'Never Enough'/'Harold & Joe' was released eventually making it to No.13 in the UK charts. 'Never Enough' was, by far, the band's most rock-orientatec track to date The usual bizarrely brilliant Tim Pope video was released to accompany the single. The video portrayed the band playing a hunchback version of the track in a tin tilting alcove. Journalist Jim Shelley was at the video shoot and noted that the only person who appeared to be having a good time was Tim Pope. Th Cure had never looked more miserabl Robert explained to Shelley whilst being hung upside down by his feet, five meters above a pool filled with shattered mirrors: "The problem is, yo can't look uncomfortable without being uncomfortable."

obert revealed in Select later: "'Never Enough' is about neve feeling satisfied with anything do. There's elements of the reactions you get to success too. That's what it's like sometimes, being stuck at the end of the pier in a freak show. It's an excellent video. It was also a play on how we could end up. I've seen other groups just acting out things on a sma stage in front of a bunch of other freaks. I wear a ball and chain, and when I fall towards the water, the thing that's holding me has saved me to put me through more years of hell."

On October 1st, the Elektra compilation album 'Rubaiyat' was released, exactly forty years after Jac Holzman started the label in his bedroom with $500, a phone and a desk.

October also saw the release of another single from the forthcoming 'Mixed Up' album, 'Close To Me'/'Just Like Heaven'. The single, like its predecessor, also made No.13 in the UK charts. Robert told Select: "I told Polydor they couldn't put this remix out as a single without a new video. It picks up where the other one left off (they had fallen off a clifftop in a wardrobe). Also Pap (Tim Pope) had done a really good under-the-sea video with Tom Tom Club, 'Oceania'. I like the video: it's really colourful and throwaway. The feeling of the original song is summed up by 'I wish I'd stayed asleep today' - the futility of it all. Sometimes you get to nine in the evening and you can't think of one decent thing you've done all day."

At the beginning of November, The Cure released 'Mixed Up' a double album of what was, essentially, dance remixes of Cure classics. The band had recruited the services of four of London's hottest DJ/producers: Mark Saunders, Paul Oakenfield, Bryan "Chuck" New and William Orbit who, among them, had been responsible for such dance faves as Neheh Cherry, Happy Mondays, Lisa Stansfield and Nitzer Ebb.

The tracks on this album included: 'Lullaby' (Ext Mix), 'Close To Me' (Closer Mix), 'Fascination Street' (Ext Mix), 'The Walk' (Everything Mix), 'Love Song' (Ext Mix), 'A Forest' (Tree Mix), 'Pictures Of You' (Ext Dub Mix), 'Hot! Hot! Hot!' (Ext Mix), 'Caterpillar' (Flicker

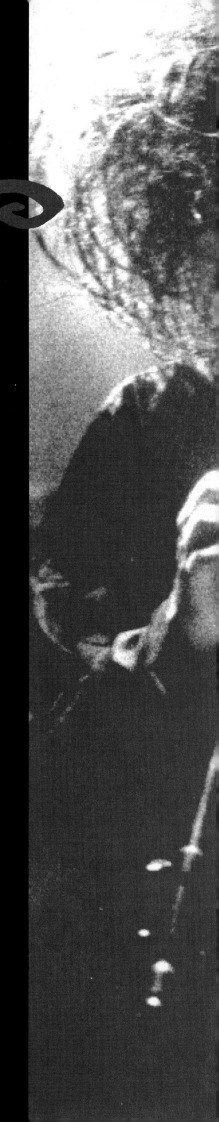

Mix), 'In Between Days' (Shiver Mix) and 'Never Enough' (Big Mix). The album was viewed with suspicion by many.

Robert explained to Lauren Spencer how the album came to be. "Well, this didn't start off to be a dance record. It started because people were trying to get a hold of old remixes and 12-inches and I saw this record collectors magazine that had the prices of singles and albums. I was having a look at what our singles were going for and I was stunned by how much they were on the market for. So, I though, the master tapes are with us, why not put them out again. Then the idea started growing into more and more of a remix album. As it turned out there aren't that many of the ones I originally wanted to do on here."

Laura Lee Davies reviewed the single: "Goths just wanna have fun! It's all very well for the B-52s to 'dance their mess around', but putting these matt-black rocksters under disco lights is quite a different matter. At first it might seem quite a pointless exercise to remix old Cure hits for the dancefloor anyway, Cure fans having quite happily shuffled their boots to 'Love Cats' and 'Let's Go To Bed' for years. However, the finished product - a few funked-up singles, radically re-recorded classics and twisted album tracks - isn't too bad, which is a tribute to original songs' strength as much as anything. It's all done with style and taste - save a few acid house touches that seem as embarrassingly unlikely as hearing

SYMBOLS

19 MORE AND WE HAVE AN ALPHABET GAME

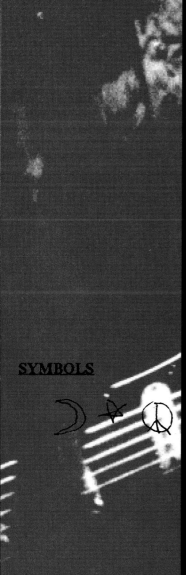

Mother Teresa telling blue jokes - but it sure is hard to imagine Robert Smith wanting to 'get down'. Unless you were inviting him to tour the deepest tomb in Highgate Cemetery, that is."

Paul Davies summed up his review in Q thus: "Long-standing Cure fans may board this particular groove train with some degree of reluctance, but overall the LP is a successful blend of experimentation and opportunism, destined to enjoy a good deal of active service on the nation's strobe-splashed dance floors."

Despite the critics' rather perplexed and guarded reactions, the album went straight into the UK charts at No.8 and made a stunning entry at No.14 in the American charts.

In an interview with Roger Morton of the NME, Robert defended the band's decision to cross over into the dance area: "I was sitting at home talking to Simon while we were doing it saying we've got to do this in a way that people don't think we're losing everyone else. I mean, the people who are on the new dance thing will be on to whatever's next, and we'll be stuck in limbo, rather than doing what we want. But unfortunately there has always been this streak through The Cure of wanting to do dance music, and it's always been there. So it's both fortunate and unfortunate that it's happened at this time, because we wanted to do it, but I think it's been pushed rather too forcefully in that direction by the record company, particularly by putting white labels into clubs."

He also revealed he is a hopeless dancer: "I seriously can't co-ordinate. For years Mary has tried to teach me the most basic co-ordination between left arm and right leg and I just cannot do it. It's alright for about three steps and then something inside my head clicks and it all goes horribly wrong.

"I used to go out to dance clubs a lot with Severin but we wouldn't dance. It'd be more like take drugs and try and get to the toilet, which would usually take about two hours. That'd be the dancing. I always used to make my way via the dancefloor and get buffeted around by people."

With Christmas 1990, The Cure expanded on their growing collection of awards. In the Sounds Readers Poll, The Cure were voted Best Live Act and Robert cleaned up in the Best Male Vocalist and Best Musician categories. 'Never Enough' won the Best Promo Video award.

Immediately after Christmas, The Cure announced they would be headlining Saturday night at the Great British Music Weekend at Wembley Arena on 19th January. Bands headlining the other days were Ozzy Osbourne and Happy Mondays. The Cure were to be supported by The Wedding Present, New Model Army, Jesus Jones, The La's and Ride. The three-day event was being held to tie in with the annual BRITS awards and was filmed by the BBC so than inserts could be screened as part of the awards TV show. The BRITS - the official British Record Industry Awards, held under the auspices of the British Phonographic Industry - were due to take place on February 10th at the London Dominion, produced by Jonathan King.

As a warm-up, the Cure played an unannounced gig at The Town & Country Club on 17th January. Billed

as 'Five Imaginary Boys', the gig was
promoted by Q, filmed by Snub TV and
supposed to be top secret. Inevitably,
the press were present in full force and
Dele Fadele was impressed: "Words
choke, trick, stupefy, have double
meanings, tie us up in knots, but they
still can't convey the dazzling brilliance
of The Cure tonight. For an institution
used to grand gestures in the stadia of
the world to pull off a low-key, 'secret
gig' with the subtlety and finesse and
make it all seem so natural, well, I'm
speechless. I don't mean to go over-
the-top but The Cure were flamboyant
and dizzying in their impact. The crystal
clear sound might've helped. But once
the first, new, barely titled song took
hold with waves of keyboards sadder
than the ocean at night resistance was
useless."

Two nights later The Cure played
Wembley. Music Week wrote: "To bill
Saturday night's event as anything
other than The Cure plus support was
to misrepresent the second evening of
the Brits weekend. Coming on last, The
Cure were the only act to life the whole
Arena to its feet, intelligently - given the
number of non-hard core fans present
opting for a singles set for their hour-
long slot."

The BRITS awards ceremony
themselves, however, didn't go quite so
well. Off-camera, Robert controversially
slammed the awards as a "farce"
despite winning the Best British Group
category at the music industry's annual
back-slapping bash. He complained
that The Cure had been used by the
BPI to heighten the awards' credibility.
He told organisers that he expressed
disappointment that the show had been
turned into "a farce", with many acts not
bothering to turn up to collect their
awards and all of the artists who were

performing, apart from The Cure, refusing to play live. One music paper wrote: "Smith insisted that the only way ahead for the BRITS was to integrate the awards into the concert weekend. And if any winning artists did not think it important enough to turn up, their awards should then be given to another nominee in the category."

arlier, during his acceptance speech, Robert snubbed Lol Tolhurst by thanking every former member of the band, by name, except for him. The series of hostilities, by all accounts, carried on at a post-awards party at The Grosvenor Hotel with a row between Robert and EMF's vocalist James Atkin sparked by remarks made by EMF about Robert's weight. A potential punch-up was narrowly avoided when Atkin apologised.

The Cure appeared in public some weeks later when they performed on Channel 4's Jonathan Ross Show and, on March 1st, they made another TV appearance, this time on MTV's Unplugged. The American programme, which was viewed by owners of satellite dishes in the UK, strips away all things electronic, leaving its featured bands to play an acoustic set. Already appearing on earlier editions of the show had been 10,000 Maniacs, The Church, Hall & Oats and Don Henley.

The Cure, true to form, took the whole idea one step further and, as well as playing acoustic guitars, pianos and bongo drums, they added a violin, harpsichord, xylophone, toy piano and four kazoos. The stage set consisted of Indian cushions, candles and joss sticks and Smith announced :"This is about the most nervous thing we've ever done."

Nervously, they played ten songs including rare live renditions of 'In Your House', 'The Blood', 'The Caterpillar', 'Letter To Elise', 'The Walk', and 'Let's Go To Bed'.

When asked if he had enjoyed the show Simon replied postively but remarked: "It's a great pity that only satellite dish owners over here will get to see the programme. I don't know anyone who's got a satellite dish and I don't know who would want one."

On March 25th, a live mini-album entitled 'Entreat' was released. The tracks were recorded during their shows at Wembley back in 1989, arguably the Cure's best-ever performances. It was first released the previous year as a limited edition CD or cassette by HMV, available as a free gift when purchasing two or more of The Cure's back catalogue. The supply was snapped up immediately by fans and copies were soon changing hands for over £20 at record fairs around the country. To put a stop to this trade, The Cure released it commercially but donated all artist royalties to ten different charities. 'Entreat' included the tracks: 'Pictures Of You', 'Closedown', 'Last Dance', 'Fascination Street', 'Prayers For Rain', 'Disintegration', 'Homesick' and 'Untitled'.

Despite the fact that the royalties were being donated to charity, the press were not impressed that another album of recycled old material had been released, following so hot on the heels of 'Mixed Up'. Robert, however, had been put in somewhat of a corner by Polydor regarding the release of 'Entreat' because the record label had been telling irate fans who couldn't obtain a copy that Robert wouldn't let them release it. Robert told Select: "I thought, if they did, all The Cure fans who were peeved before are now going to hate my guts."

On July 8th The Cure released 'Picture Show - An Improbable Collection', a compilation video charting the course of the collaboration between The Cure and Tim Pope.

'Picture Show' opened with Robert explaining to a young TV presenter that the video for 'Why Can't I Be You' was inspired by Five Star's dance routines. The compilation included the videos for 'Why Can't I Be You?' (12"), 'Catch', 'Hot Hot Hot!!!' (12"), 'Just Like Heaven', 'Lullaby', 'Fascination Street', 'Love Song', 'Pictures Of You', 'Never Enough' and 'Close To Me' (Closer Mix). Nick Griffiths reviewed 'Picture Show': "Between their first, endearing promo video collection, 'Staring At The Sea', and this, their latest instalment, The Cure have developed into a soap opera for their seemingly close-knit members. No band has stuck so fervently to an image for so long. Sadly, no one has taught them lipstick application, the merits of hair hygiene, clothes sense or alcohol abstinence. And still they are quietly huge, lapping up stadiums world-wide.

"'Picture Show' takes in the singles from 1987's 'Kiss Me, Kiss Me, Kiss Me' to last year's 'Mixed Up' remix album, all directed by Tim Pope. Effectively the band's sixth member, Pope was born with a video in his hand and a colourful, surreal imagination. Rather than directing, he places. The success of these later videos rest not so much in what happens at the start, at the end and in between as in their uncannily perfect locations. How did he

know to have 'Just Like Heaven' take place atop a cliff and 'Love Song' in a cave of chocolate stalagmites?

"The Cure, and Smith in particular, manage to gain and shed weight and hair miraculously. In the duration of two 'Kiss Me' videos, Smith and Tolhurst swop 20lbs of excess weight between each other, and the singer's hair grows a foot. Their recording career might be lucrative, but if they could market their weight-gain and hair-loss cures, The Cure would never need to work again."

o tie in with the release of 'Picture Show', The Cure also released their entire back catalogue as a special box set. Entitled 'Assemblage', the beautifully packaged set included the albums 'Three Imaginary Boys', 'Boys Don't Cry', 'Seventeen Seconds', 'Faith', 'Pornography', 'Japanese Whispers', 'The Top', 'Concert', 'The Head On The Door', 'Standing On A Beach', 'Kiss Me, Kiss Me, Kiss Me' and 'Disintegration'. The release of both of these products, however, was marred by an unpleasant legal wrangle between Robert and Lol. A week before the release, Robert had received a letter from Lol's lawyers informing him that there were proceeding with court action. Apparently, Lol claimed that he was entitled to more money for his contribution to The Cure. Robert was flabbergasted and told Select: "It's really stupid. He'll lose and he'll have to pay costs and it'll cost him more than he could hope to win. And he's going to lose any credibility he had as regards what he did in The Cure, because it'll all come out...."

Robert also revealed to Select that Lol was unable to cope musically from the very beginning. He did, however, attempt the drumming for a while but was unable to master the disco beat of 'Let's Go To Bed'. "I did them on my own and Lol was just there for company, basically. I was spending late nights in the studio and he was just someone who'd sit there and I'd talk to. When we did 'Let's Go To Bed' he tried to do the drumbeat for it for about three days, and it cost us a fortune in studio time. In the end we got in a session drummer. He was going to pretend he'd played it until I pointed out to him that if he had to play it somewhere and he couldn't he'd be humiliated."

In August, The Cure went into the studio to commence recording an eagerly-awaited new album, managing to stay completely out of the glare of the media spotlight whilst they did so. Little was heard of the band until November, when they broke their silence by releasing another video compilation, entitled 'The Cure Play Out'. Running at 124 minutes, the video combined live footage of the band with a behind-the-scenes insight covering a month in the life of The Cure. The live footage offered versions of four hitherto unreleased tracks: 'Wendy Time, 'The Big Hand', 'Away' and 'A Letter To Elise' taken from the secret gig at the Town And Country Club and their headlining performance at Wembley Arena during the Great British Music Weekend. The more intimate moments are taken from various soundchecks, rehearsals, record company meetings and interviews.

One publication wrote: "It could be argued by uncharitable souls that 'Play Out' goes a wee bit too far with the in-between stuff - there are only so many times you can watch the band walk into buildings without the excitement wearing off slightly. But there are numerous gems, and 'Play Out' certainly does give an idea of life in The Cure. It also gives us a surreal, incomprehensible conversation about losing an arm in a helicopter accident." At Christmas, despite not having released any new product for two years, The Cure still featured strongly in the Melody Maker Readers' Poll. They won the Best Music Video category for 'Picture Show' and Robert hung on to his title of Best Male Artist. In addition to this, Robert's name appeared in the new edition of high society who's who - Debrett's. He listed his hobbies as "deep-sea diving, hot air ballooning, reading, writing, and looking into space." Even Debrett's couldn't coax him to tell the truth.

1992 could be the biggest year yet for The Cure. They have a single 'High'/'The Twilight Garden' scheduled for release on 9th March and an album entitled 'Wish' due out on 13th April. Rumour has it that they also have a lengthy world tour currently in the planning stage, scotching any further speculation that The Cure have quit from the live scene.

Having sold over ten million albums, they have gradually become one of the biggest-selling acts in the world. How much bigger can they get or, indeed, how much bigger do they want to get?

Robert recently told Hello: "Oh, I'm not up there with the megastars and nor would I like to be. We'd rather keep our original audience and expand it where possible than sell-out to a more fickle crowd. Mind you, that doesn't mean I have any objection to the postman humming our tunes in the morning."

WRITTEN ON ME BUS GOING HOME...

all word association by robert courtesy of the cure fan club

At some time during our lives, most of us become slightly obsessed with a particular band or pop star. Posters go up on bedroom walls, albums are collected and videos are watched repeatedly. But for twenty-seven year old Chris White, his obsession with The Cure and, particularly, Robert Smith, runs deeper.

Working as a CD buyer for Caroline International, a record export company owned by the Virgin Group of Companies, his job enables him to expand on his vast collection of Cure releases and he avidly snaps up limited editions and special formats. However, on meeting Chris, a softly spoken, polite young man, it is immediately apparent that his infatuation with The Cure has become less of an obsession and more a way of life.

His dark hair is teased and gelled into an exact replica of Smith's own, he dresses in Smith's uniform of baggy jumpers, tight black jeans and huge trainers, he knows more about The Cure than they probably do themselves and is currently going out with Janie who runs the Cure's fan club, although he is quick to point out that it is their mutual admiration for the band that brought them together and he does not view her as part of his 'collection'. In addition, he spends his entire annual vacation, and his savings, following The Cure on tour, wherever that might lead. That is true devotion and this is his story.

A FAN'S EYE VIEW

The first time I heard The Cure was in 1982. I saw a poster for the 'Pornography' album in my local record shop and was curious enough to buy the record. I realised immediately that The Cure were everything I was looking for in a band, both musically and lyrically. I have been a devoted fan ever since, but 'Pornography' will always be my favourite album.

I have accumulated a vast collection of Cure memorabilia - all record releases including special formats and limited editions, T-shirts, books, posters, videos and magazine cuttings from around the world including Brazil, Japan and America.

But the best part of all are the concerts. I have been to many throughout Europe and to every show in the UK since 1985. This year I plan to go to America and take in as much of the European tour as my money and holidays will allow.

I STILL, AND SUPPOSE ALWAYS WILL, SEE
...EETING ARCHAIC IMAGES SUCH AS EXIST IN
...L OLD CHRISTIAN PAINTINGS—
(BUT THESE ETERNAL FIRES ARE S...
PUT OUT BY AN INFINITY
OF NOTHINGNESS.
ie. I DON'T BELIEVE IN
HELL !!

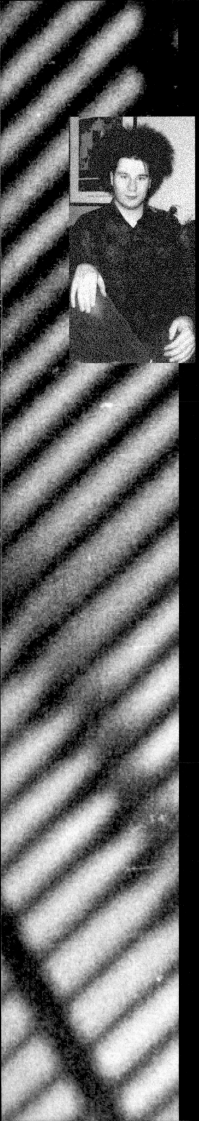

Chris White

My personal favourite Cure events over the past ten years are:
The first listen to a new album or single, I always experience an unexpected feeling or mood.

The Greenpeace concert at The Royal Albert Hall in 1986 - the first time I heard them play the song 'Faith' when we all cried.

The 'Prayer' tour for the album 'Disintegration - especially the shows in Paris, Birmingham and the last night of the tour in London when they played for over three hours.

The 'Five Imaginary Boys' secret gig at the Town and Country in January 1991

Being one of the very few Cure fans in the invited audience for the filming of MTV's 'Unplugged'.

One of the main attractions of The Cure, in my opinion, is their ability to cross musical boundaries without ever conforming. They do what they believe in, never compromising for the sake of commercial success, and have fun doing it. Many older Cure fans claimed they had 'sold out' with the release of 'Let's Go To Bed', 'The Walk' and 'The Love Cats', however, during that time they gained many new fans. The following album 'The Top' was a complete U-turn in musical direction and perhaps not a good decision commercially but it was The Cure doing what they believed in and it worked.

Many people have tried to categorise The Cure over the years, calling them punk, pop, new wave, moody, Goth and even, at the time, "the Pink Floyd of the Eighties!" yet they don't fit into any one category. In my mind this is an unique achievement.

Most artists who achieve as much success as that of The Cure become 'prima donas but The Cure have always had their feet firmly on the ground and have never lost touch with their roots. As individuals, they have remained untouched by fame, still living in modest homes and driving normal cars, shunning the 'champagne and caviar' lifestyle.

I have been asked to list my favourite songs but they never remain the same from day to day, due to the fact that when my mood changes so does my favourite song. However, today they are:

'A Figurehead' from 'Pornography'
'Just Like Heaven' from 'Kiss Me Kiss Me Kiss Me'
'Faith' - any live version from 1989
'Love Song from 'Disintegration'
'Sinking' from 'The Head On The Door'
'A Forest' - live 1981-91
'M' from 'Seventeen Seconds'
'Charlotte Sometimes' - a single between albums

The end, but not really......!

THE CURE OFFICIAL DISCOGRAPHY

UK SINGLES

Title	Format	Cat. No.
A forest/another journey by train	7"	fics 010
A forest/another journey by train	12"	ficx 010
Boys don't cry/pillbox tales/do the hansa	12"	ficsx24
Boys don't cry/pillbox tales	7"	fics 24
Boys don't cry/plastic passion	7"	fics 002
Catch/breath (picture disc)	7"	ficsp26
Catch/breath/kyoto song (live)/a night like this (live)	12"	ficse26
Catch/breath	7"	fics 26
Catch/breath/a chain of flowers	12"	ficsx26
Catch/breath/a chain of flowers	cassette	ficsc26
Charlotte sometimes/splintered in her head/faith	12"	ficx 14
Charlotte sometimes/splintered in her head	7"	fics 14
Close to me (remix)/a man inside my mouth (poster)	7"	ficsg23
Close to me (remix)/a man inside my mouth/new day/stop dead	10"	ficst23
Close to me (remix)/a man inside my mouth	7"	fics 23
Close to me/just like heaven	cassette	ficcs36
Close to me/just like heaven	cd	ficcd36
Close to me/just like heaven/primary	12"	ficsx36
Close to me/just like heaven	7"	fics 36
Close to me (ext.remix)/a man inside my mouth/stop dead	12"	ficsx23
Hot hot hot! (ext. remix)/hot hot hot! (remix)/hey you	12"	ficsx28
Hot hot hot! (ext. remix)/hot hot hot! (remix)/hey you	cd	ficsx28
I'm a cult hero/I dig you ("Cult Hero")	7"	fics 006
In between days/the exploding boy	7"	fics 22
In between days/the exploding boy/a few hours after	12"	ficsx22
Jumping someone else's train/I'm cold	7"	fics 005
Just like heaven (remix)/snow in summer (picture disc)	7"	fics 27
Just like heaven (remix)/snow in summer/sugar girl	7"	ficcd27
Just like heaven (remix)/snow in summer/sugar girl	12"	ficsx27
Just like heaven (remix)/snow in summer	7"	fics 27
Killing an arab/10.15 Saturday night	7"	fics 001
Killing an arab/10.15 Saturday night	7"	small 11
Let's go to bed/just one kiss	12"	ficsx17
Let's go to bed/just one kiss	7"	fics 17
Love song/2 late	7"	fics 30
Love song/2 late ("the love box")	7"	ficsg30
Love song/2 late/fear of ghosts/love song (ext.remix)	12"	ficsx30
Love song/2 late/fear of ghosts/love song (ext.remix)	cd	ficcd30
Love song/2 late	cassette	ficcs30
Lullaby (remix)/babble (clear vinyl)	7"	ficsp29
Lullaby (remix)/babble (gatefold sleeve)	7"	ficsg29
Lullaby (ext.remix)/babble/out of mind	12"	ficsx29
Lullaby (ext.remix)/babble/out of mind (pink vinyl)	12"	ficvx29
Lullaby (remix)/babble/out of mind/lullaby (ext.remix)	3"cd	ficcd29
Lullaby (remix)/babble	7"	fics 29
Never enough/harold and joe	cassette	ficcs35
Never enough (big mix)/harold and joe/let's go to bed	12"	ficsx35
Never enough/harold and joe	7"	fics 35
Never enough (big mix)/harold and joe/let's go to bed	cd	ficcd35
Pictures of you (remix)/last dance (green vinyl)	7"	ficpa34
Pictures of you (ext.remix)/last dance/fascination st.(grn.)	12"	fixpa34
Pictures of you (ext.remix)/last dance/fascination st.	12"	ficxa34
Pictures of you (remix)/last dance	7"	fica 34
Pictures of you (remix)/prayers for rain (purple vinyl)	7"	ficpb34
Pictures of you (remix)/prayers for rain	7"	ficb 34
Pictures of you (ext.remix)/last dance/fascination st.	cd	ficda34
Pictures of you (remix)/last dance	cassette	ficca34
Pictures of you(strangemix)/prayers for rain/disintegration	12"	ficxb34
Pictures of you(strangemix)/prayers for rain/disint. (purp.)	12"	fixpb34
Pictures of you (ext.remix)/prayers for rain/disint.	cd	ficdb34
Pictures of you (ext.remix)/prayers for rain	cassette	ficcb34
Primary (ext)/descent	12"	ficx 012
Primary/descent	7"	fics 012
The hanging garden/100 years/a forest/killing an arab	7" x 2	ficg 15
The hanging garden/100 years	7"	fics 15
The lovecats/speak my language	7"	fics 19
The lovecats/speak my language (picture disc)	7"	ficsp19
The walk/the dream	7"	fics 18
The walk/the dream (picture disc)	7"	ficsp18
The walk/the dream/the upstairs room/lament	12"	ficsx18
The caterpillar/happy the man/throw your foot	12"	ficsx20
The Peel session	12"	sfps050
The caterpillar/happy the man (picture disc)	7"	ficsp20
The Peel session	cd	sfpscd050
The caterpillar/happy the man	7"	fics 20
The lovecats (ext)/speak my language/mr. pink eyes	12"	ficsx19
Why can't I be you?/a japanese dream/6 diff. ways/push	7"x2	ficsg25
Why can't I be you? (remix)/a japanese dream	12"	ficsx25
Why can't I be you?/a Japanese dream	7"	fics 25

THE CURE OFFICIAL DISCOGRAPHY
ALBUMS

Three imaginary boys 1979	album	fix1
	cassette	fixc1
	cd	827 686-2
Seventeen seconds 1980	album	fix4
	cassette	fixc4
	cd	825 364-2
Faith 1981	album	fix6
	cassette	fixc6
	cd	827 687-2
Pornography 1982	album	fixd7
	cassette	fixdc7
	cd	827 688-2
Boys don't cry 1983	album	spelp26
	cassette	spemc26
	cd	815 011-2
Japanese whispers 1983	album	fixm 8
	cassette	fixmc8
	cd	817 470-2
The top 1984	album	fixs 9
	cassette	fixmc9
	cd	821 136-2
Concert -		
The cure live/curiosity '77-'88	album	fixh 10
	cassette	fixhc10
	cd	823 682-2
The head on the door 1985	album	fixh 11
	cassette	fixhc11
	cd	827 231-2
Standing on a beach/		
staring at the sea	album	fixh 12
	cassette	fixhc12
	cd	829 239-2
Kiss me kiss me kiss me 1987	double album	fixh 13
	cassette	fixhc13
	cd	832 130-2
Kiss me kiss me kiss me		
1987(Dec.) with 12" orange e.p.	album only	fixha13
Disintegration 1989	album	fixh 14
	cassette	fixhc14
	cd	839 353-2
	Picture disc '90	841 946-1
Mixed up	album	847 009-1
	cassette	847 009-4
	cd	847 009-2
Mixed up (Ltd.Ed.) 5 Picture cd's	cd only	867 529-5
Entreat 1991	album	fixlp 17
	cassette	fixcs 17
	cd	fixcd 17
Assemblage Box set	cd	511 124-2

222

THE CURE BOOTLEG DISCOGRAPHY

A day like this	double L.P.
A day like this	double L.P.
Accuracy (Lille '81)	2cd
Aids	double L.P.
All cure	
Arabian dream	
Arabian dream	(multi-coloured vinyl)
Arabian dream	(coloured vinyl)
Arboreal	double L.P.
After the cure I'm alive and well	
All the love cats are grey	(coloured vinyl)
A night like this	
Baby scream	double L.P.
BBC transcription	
Behind closed doors	
Birmingham (wall rec.)	
The blood screw	7"
Blue sunshine (with glove)	
Boys don't cry (promo)	
Carnage visors	
Charlotte sometimes (promo)	
Crystal palace 11/8/90 vol 1 (austr)	cd
Crystal palace 11/8/90 vol 2 (austr)	cd
Cult hero	7"
Cure (fuctoni rec.) (with poster)	
Cure (primary)	
Dark night the prayer (glr)	2cd
Difficult to cure (beecm) Birm. 22/5/88	cd
Dressed up again (host) Roskilde 30/6/88	double L.P.
Dressing up	double L.P.
Difficult to cure UK '88	live cd
Elephant's grind	double L.P.
Entreat	live cd
Entreat Wembley '88	(8 tracks) promo cd
Entreat	(re-release)
European tour '85	live cd
Fading roots	double L.P.
Final romance	(coloured vinyl)
Final romance	re-release (multi-coloured vinyl)
Fireheads	
Fireheads	(coloured vinyl)
Five imaginary boys '91 (robin)	cd
Full moon concert (swing) Leysin fest. 7/6/90	double L.P.
Full moon concert (swing) Leysin fest. 7/6/90	2Cd
Getting old	
Girls don't cry (host) Berlin.& Neth. '79/80	double L.P.
Glastonbury '90 (austr)	cd
The grave which grins at last	
The head on the door (spock rec.)	double L.P.
Hot	triple L.P.
Hot hot hot (redph) Torino '89	2cd
I'm a cult hero/i dig you (stamp)	(with 7" & book)
I-beam	double L.P.
Imaginary boys/songs	(picture disc) live cd
In concert	
In concert '80	live cd
In concert Glastonbury '86 (BBC transcription disc)	
In concert Glastonbury '86 (bootleg)	
Incureble	
In the beginning	double L.P.
Invasion of the bodysnatchers	double L.P.
John peel session '81	e.p.
Kiss me for cure (rocla)	
The 'kissing' tour '87	double L.P.
The 'kissing' tour '87	(picture disc) double **L.P.**
The 'kissing' tour '87	live 2cd
Kiss me kiss me kiss me (observation rec.)	double L.P.
Kiss me kiss me kiss me	(with orange vinyl12") triple L.P.
Kyoto songs	double L.P.
L.A. Forum '87	double L.P.
Let's go	(with postcard)
Live	(red poster cover)

Live	(yellow poster cover)
Live at the NEC, Birmingham '85	
Live at the Paradiso Amsterdam 12/12/79	
Live at the funeral party	double L.P.
Live in Berlin '85	double L.P.
Live in Bremen '87	double L.P.
Live in Brussels '80	live cd
Live in Bologna 20/5/84	(picture disc)
Live in Essen '89	double L.P.
Live in Germany	
Live in Italy	(picture disc)
Live in Milan at the rolling stone	double L.P.
Live in Milan at the rolling stone 1 (picture disc)	
Live in Milan at the rolling stone 2 (picture disc)	
Live in Sydney '80	cd
Live on prospect hill '80 (c1/c2)	double L.P.
Live on prospect hill '80 (diff)	re-release
double **L.P.**	
Live on prospect hill	(picture disc) live 2cd
Looking for a forest	
"M" Paris '82	(with cd single) live cd
Madness	double L.P.
Manifest	
1985 Europe tour (golds)	double L.P.
No cure to pay	double L.P.
One more holy hour	
Outer walls	double L.P.
Play for today (swing)	(multi-coloured vinyl) double **L.P.**
Play for today Arnheim '80	double L.P.
Play for today Arnheim '80	live cd
Pornography (promo)	
Pornography tour	
Pornography tour	double L.P.
Pornography tour Paris '82	live cd
Pretty baby scream	triple L.P.
Promary production	
Promotional	double L.P.
Radio show 9/11/87	live cd
Sinking with love	
Sorry Robert we can't stop (specials)	double L.P.
Sorry Robert we can't stop (specials)	(coloured vinyl) double **L.P.**
Sorry Robert we can't stop (specials) vol.2	
Sorry Robert we can't stop (specials) vol.2	(coloured vinyl)
Sorry Robert we can't stop (specials) vol.3	double L.P.
Sorry Robert we can't stop (specials) vol.3	(coloured vinyl) double L.P.
The spell's unbroken	
The spell's unbroken	(coloured vinyl)
Stiff as toys	
Stranger than fiction	(3 unrel tracks) promo c.D.
Swingin' piggy in the mirror	cd
Three imaginary boys	
Torture UK '87	live cd
Town & country club 17/1/91	live cd
U.K. 1987 (Golds)	cd
Vintage concert radio series	live cd
Visions of domino	
Visions of domino	(coloured vinyl)
The walk UK tour '87	live cd
We hate rock 'n' roll Neth.(Pyram)	cd
Wembley arena '85	double L.P.
Wembley arena live '85	live cd
Yellow mood	

three imaginary boys • boys don't cry • seventeen
seconds • faith • pornography• concert • the top •
japanese whispers • head on the door • standing on a
beach • kiss me kiss me kiss me • disintegration